A SONG for ALL SEASONS

A SONG for ALL SEASONS

25 Hymn Stories Celebrating
God, Home, and Country

KENNETH W.
OSBECK

Kregel
Publications

A Song for All Seasons: 25 Hymn Stories Celebrating God, Home, and Country

© 2003 by Kenneth W. Osbeck

Published by Kregel Publications, a division of Kregel, Inc., P.O. Box 2607, Grand Rapids, MI 49501.

Library of Congress Cataloging-in-Publication Data
Osbeck, Kenneth W.
A song for all seasons: 25 hymn stories celebrating God, home, and country / by Kenneth W. Osbeck.
   p. cm.
  1. Hymns, English—United States—History and criticism.
2. Holidays—United States. I. Title.
BV313.O745   2003
264'.23—dc21   2003001783

ISBN 0-8254-3350-9

Printed in the United States of America

03 04 05 06 07 / 5 4 3 2 1

As we commemorate our nation's
most recent observance,
Patriot Day,
honoring those who died
as a result of the
September 11, 2001, terrorist attacks,
may we never forget those who perished
and those who gave their lives
with courage and self-sacrifice.

In God we trust!
United we stand!
Proud to be an American!
Committed to Christ and His transforming gospel!

Freedom is to democracy what air is to fire, an element without which it instantly expires.

—James Madison

Contents

Introduction

> If my people, who are called by my name, will humble them-
> selves and pray and seek my face and turn from their wicked
> ways, then will I hear from heaven and will forgive their sin
> and will heal their land.
>
> —2 Chronicles 7:14

Since earliest recorded times, people around the world have celebrated special event days in the history of their countries. These
national holidays and celebrations portray a nation at its best—
its triumphs and causes to be remembered, and its values and
memories to be cherished. May this now be true of the most
recent eventful day—September 11—a day for honoring those
who died as a result of the treacherous terrorist attacks. September 11, 2001, was a day that stunned and shook the American
people as they have never before been shaken. Until that time we
did not realize that we could be so vulnerable. It was also a day
that brought American citizens to a new level of patriotic loyalty
and awoke an indomitable spirit of determination to see the evils
of global terrorism eliminated.

An awareness and appreciation of our nation's special days
should lead to a grateful reflection on the true meaning of
these historic events. These days should also serve as reminders to
humbly respond to God with prayer and praise for all of His past
blessings, and to earnestly seek His continued guidance for the
future.

For a Christian, *praying* (communing) and *praising* (glorifying) are two of the most vital spiritual pursuits in a life committed to the will of God. Scripture provides this important instruction:

> I will *pray* with the *spirit,* and I will pray with the *understanding* also: I will *sing* with the *spirit,* and I will sing with the *understanding* also.
>
> —1 Corinthians 14:15 (KJV, emphasis added)

Praying with the spirit and with understanding—

In everything, by prayer and petition, with thanksgiving, present your requests to God.

—Philippians 4:6

- Pray for wise decision-making by our president and the leaders of our government.
- Pray for a genuine return to the Christian principles on which this nation was founded.
- Pray for the spiritual wisdom of fellow believers in ministering effectively for God during these days of unusual opportunity.
- Pray for our families, that they will remain morally steadfast during these unsettling times.

And let there be praise!

Whoso offereth praise glorifieth me [God].

—Psalm 50:23 (KJV)

Teach and admonish one another with all wisdom, and as you sing psalms, hymns and spiritual songs [do it] with gratitude in your hearts to God.

—Colossians 3:16

Through Jesus, therefore, let us continually offer to God a sacrifice of praise—the fruit of lips that confess his name.

—Hebrews 13:15

- Praise that America still stands united as "the land of the free and the home of the brave," despite the vicious terrorist attacks by those bent on our destruction.
- Praise for the many freedoms that still are ours to enjoy.
- Praise for the opportunity to represent our Lord at this historic time.

In the aftermath of September 11, when there is still much unrest throughout our land, may we as the people of God determine to model Christ's love, compassion, and joy to a disturbed society. This is an appropriate time for each Christian to ponder seriously these words of Scripture:

Who knoweth whether thou art come to the kingdom for such a time as this?

—Esther 4:14 (KJV)

This challenging question was first posed to Queen Esther during a bleak period when the Jewish people were held captive by a ruthless Persian Empire intent on their destruction. But God heard the cry of His people and providentially intervened.

Then may we accept the challenge given in the seventeenth century to the early settlers of our land by one of the leaders of the great migration to America:

> We shall be a city upon a hill. We must rise to our responsibilities and learn to live as God intended men to live: In charity, love and cooperation with one another—to live in accord with a Biblical ethic.
>
> —John Winthrop
> A founder of the Massachusetts Bay Colony

And the command of Christ Himself:
> Let your light shine before men, that they may see your good deeds and praise your Father in heaven.
>
> —Matthew 5:16

And this biblical charge by the apostle Paul:

> So that you may become blameless and pure, children of God without fault in a crooked and depraved generation, in which you shine like stars in the universe as you hold out the word of life.
>
> —Philippians 2:15–16

Whatever makes men good Christians also makes them good citizens.
> —Daniel Webster

❖ ❖ ❖

I'm gonna live so God can use me, anywhere, any time;
I'm gonna live so God can use me, anywhere, Lord, any time;
I'm gonna work so God can use me, anywhere, any time;
I'm gonna work so God can use me, anywhere, Lord, any time;
I'm gonna pray so God can use me, anywhere, any time;
I'm gonna pray so God can use me, anywhere, Lord, any time;
I'm gonna sing so God can use me, anywhere, any time;
I'm gonna sing so God can use me, anywhere, Lord, any time.

—Spiritual

While the storm clouds gather
far across the sea,
Let us swear allegiance to a land
that's free.
Let us all be grateful for a land so fair,
As we raise our voices in a solemn prayer.

God bless America, land that I love.
Stand beside her and guide her
Thru the night with a light from above.
From the mountains, to the prairies,
To the oceans white with foam.
God bless America, my home sweet home.
God bless America, my home sweet home.

The Power of a Song

Give me the making of the songs of a nation, and I care not who makes its laws.

—Andrew Fletcher, 1655–1716

"God Bless America"

—Irving Berlin, 1888–1989

Since the September 11 terrorist attacks, the singable lyrics of "God Bless America" have once again stirred the patriotic responses of the American people, just as they did during the bleak days of World War II.

In 1938, when ominous war clouds were gathering across the sea, Kate Smith, one of this country's all-time favorite singers, asked Irving Berlin to write a song especially for her Armistice Day broadcast. Berlin found one that he had written previously for an Army soldier show during World War I, but the song had never been used. Kate Smith introduced it on her Armistice Day radio program, and it became her signature song throughout the war years of the 1940s. Later, Bing Crosby's recording of the song became a best-seller. In 1954, President Eisenhower awarded a citation of merit to Irving Berlin as the composer of "God Bless America" and other patriotic songs that had contributed much to the morale of our people.

Irving Berlin was born in Russia on May 11, 1888. As an infant he was brought to the United States and was raised in New York's lower east side. He rose from a humble childhood to a life of fame and wealth as the composer of more than one thousand songs during his lifetime of 101 years. Berlin continued to write musical comedies, climaxing his career with the very successful "Annie, Get Your Gun." His music is said to have influenced every popular singer, songwriter, and composer of the twentieth century. Irving Berlin always felt that "God Bless America" was the most important song he had written. He loved to sing it himself, especially during his later years when he would express great emotion about the land he loved. The song was a sincere "thank you" to a country that had given a poor immigrant boy an opportunity to become successful.

Like many of our timeless hymns and favorite songs, "God Bless America" doesn't wear thin with time and usage. Today it is still sung with passion by those of every age in schools, in houses of worship, at athletic events, and wherever people gather to extol the "land that I love."

As we sing Irving Berlin's inspiring song, may we not only ask God to bless our land, but may we in turn be directed to bless Almighty God. May it be our earnest concern that our nation ever be worthy of His divine blessing.

How good it is to sing praises to our God, how pleasant and fitting to praise him!

—Psalm 147:1

New Year's Day

~

I asked the New Year for some motto sweet,
Some rule of life, by which to guide my feet.
I asked and paused; it answered soft and low,
God's will to know.

—Author Unknown

This is the only holiday celebrated by the entire world. Celebrations differ greatly, however, from raucous frolics ushering in the New Year to more serious reflections by those who seek to replace the failures of the past with new resolve for the future. The ability to begin a renewed life is one of the major themes of the Bible:

> "Come now, let us reason together," says the LORD. "Though your sins are like scarlet, they shall be as white as snow; though they are red as crimson, they shall be like wool."
>
> —Isaiah 1:18

> Therefore, if anyone is in Christ, he is a new creation; the old is gone, the new has come!
>
> —2 Corinthians 5:17

Poet Alfred Tennyson expressed the possibility of personal renewal with these lines:

> I hold it truth with him who sings
> To one clear harp on divers tones,
> That men may rise on stepping stones
> Of their dead selves to higher things.

During the Middle Ages, various countries began the new year on different dates. In 1582, Pope Gregory XIII decreed that January 1 was to be the official New Year's Day throughout the Western world. In 1752, January 1 was designated as the official holiday in the United States and Great Britain.

It should be noted that January 1, 1863, was a most memorable day in American history. It was on this day that President Abraham Lincoln issued his historic Emancipation Proclamation, declaring that all slaves would henceforth be free. Two years later, the Thirteenth Amendment legally abolished slavery throughout the land. This was an important time of moral renewal in our country.

Prayer

I with Thee would begin, O my Savior so dear, on the way that I still must pursue; I with Thee would begin every day granted here, as my earnest resolve I renew—to be and remain Thine forever. Amen.

—From the Swedish

And let there be praise!

Savior, like a shepherd lead us,
Much we need Thy tender care;
In Thy pleasant pastures feed us,
For our use Thy folds prepare:
Blessed Jesus, blessed Jesus,
Thou hast bought us, Thine we are.

We are Thine—do Thou befriend us,
Be the guardian of our way;
Keep Thy flock, from sin defend us,
Seek us when we go astray:
Blessed Jesus, blessed Jesus,
Hear, O hear us when we pray.

Thou hast promised to receive us,
Poor and sinful tho we be;
Thou hast mercy to relieve us,
Grace to cleanse and pow'r to free:
Blessed Jesus, blessed Jesus,
Early let us turn to Thee.

Early let us seek Thy favor,
Early let us do Thy will;
Blessed Lord and only Savior,
With Thy love our bosoms fill:
Blessed Jesus, blessed Jesus,
Thou hast loved us, love us still.

Savior, Like a
Shepherd Lead Us

I will instruct you and teach you in the way you should go;
I will counsel you and watch over you.

—Psalm 32:8

*B*ecoming a Christian is a thrilling experience—when one initially trusts in the finished work of Christ and realizes that he now has a new and perfect relationship with his Creator. There is also the glorious hope of spending an endless eternity with God in heaven. But one of the real blessings of the Christian life is simply to awaken each day—to begin a new faith adventure with the Lord—and to realize with childlike trust that my all-knowing heavenly Father is guiding each step I take.

The Bible equates being guided by the Spirit of God with being a child of God (Rom. 8:14). Yet, even as our natural children can sometimes rebel against parental authority, so we too can forsake God's leading in our lives and seek our own ways. With implicit faith we must believe that God has a planned path for each of His children, and we must deeply desire to follow that path wherever it leads. With the psalmist David we can say:

He makes me lie down in green pastures,
he leads me beside quiet waters,
he restores my soul.

—Psalm 23:2–3

Dorothy Thrupp, author of this well-known hymn, was born and resided in London, England. She was a prolific writer of children's hymns and devotional materials, although she seldom signed her name to any of her works. When she did sign a composition, she would use a pseudonym. For this reason, it has never fully been proven that she was the actual author of "Savior, Like a Shepherd Lead Us," although the hymn first appeared in 1836—unsigned—in her collection *Hymns for the Young*.

The composer of the music for "Savior, Like a Shepherd Lead Us" was William Bradbury, an important American contributor to the development of early gospel music in this country. Bradbury has supplied the music for such other favorites as "Just As I Am," "The Solid Rock," "He Leadeth Me," and "Sweet Hour of Prayer." Bradbury is also considered a pioneer in music for children—in the church and in the public schools. He is credited with being the promoter of the music education program in the New York City schools. Bradbury also published more than fifty books of music collections throughout his productive lifetime.

Throughout the new year, may we be sensitive to and confident of God's inner voice of guidance. May we be willing followers wherever the path may lead.

Whether you turn to the right or to the left, your ears will hear a voice behind you, saying, "This is the way; walk in it."
—Isaiah 30:21

"For I know the plans I have for you," declares the LORD, "plans to prosper you and not to harm you, plans to give you hope and a future."

—Jeremiah 29:11

Guide me, O Thou great Jehovah,
    Pilgrim thru this barren land;
I am weak, but Thou art mighty—
    Hold me with Thy pow'rful hand:
Bread of Heaven, Bread of Heaven,
    Feed me till I want no more,
    Feed me till I want no more.

Open now the crystal fountain
Whence the healing stream doth flow;
    Let the fire and cloudy pillar
    Lead me all my journey thru:
Strong Deliv'rer, strong Deliv'rer,
Be Thou still my strength and shield,
Be Thou still my strength and shield.

When I tread the verge of Jordan,
    Bid my anxious fears subside;
Bear me thru the swelling current,
    Land me safe on Canaan's side:
Songs of praises, songs of praises
    I will ever give to Thee,
    I will ever give to Thee.

Guide Me, O Thou
Great Jehovah

He [the Lord] guides the humble in what is right
and teaches them his way.

—Psalm 25:9

*T*he dawn of a new year reminds us anew that the need for daily guidance is one of our chief concerns. "Guide Me, O Thou Great Jehovah" is one of the finest hymns of the church on this theme. How easily our lives can go astray without the awareness of divine leadership.

During the early part of the eighteenth century, a young Welsh preacher, Howell Harris, was stirring Wales with his evangelistic preaching and congregational singing. (Throughout the centuries, the Welsh have been recognized as some of the most enthusiastic singers in the world.) In England, the Wesley brothers, John and Charles, were conducting similar revivals and outdoor campaigns. William Williams is one who was touched by Harris's preaching. Prior to this time, Williams had been preparing for the medical profession. But upon hearing a sermon by Harris, young Williams gave his heart and life to God and decided to enter the ministry.

Williams served two parishes in the Anglican Church for a time, but never felt at ease with its ritualistic services. Like Harris, he decided to adopt all of Wales as his parish, and for the next forty-three years he traveled nearly one hundred thousand miles on horseback, preaching and singing the gospel in his native tongue. Though he suffered many hardships in his long itinerant ministry, including attacks and beatings by mobs, William Williams became affectionately known as the "sweet singer of Wales." He was highly respected as a persuasive preacher, yet his greatest contributions were his hymns—approximately eight hundred of them, all in the Welsh language. Unfortunately, most of these texts have not been translated.

The imagery of "Guide Me, O Thou Great Jehovah" is drawn wholly from the Bible. The forty-year desert journey of the Israelites is compared to the pilgrimage of the Christian life toward our heavenly home—a "pilgrim through this barren land." Note the picturesque expressions used throughout: "bread of heaven" (daily manna), "crystal fountain" (the pure, crystalline stream that flowed from the rock), "fire and cloudy pillar" (daily guidance), "Jordan" (death itself), "Canaan's side" (heaven's eternity).

The strong symbolic text, combined with its virile music, has had great universal appeal, evidenced by the fact that the hymn has been translated into more than seventy-five languages. The text with this robust "CWM Rhondda" tune, composed in 1907 for the annual Baptist singing festival at Capel Rhondda, Wales, is still one of the most popular and widely used hymns in Wales. It is not uncommon even today for a crowd at a public event to burst forth into the spontaneous singing of this hymn.

As we reflect on the truths of this text, may we acquire new insights about God's guidance, even as the Israelites did in their forty-year wilderness journey. May our daily prayer be that of the psalmist: "Since you are my rock and my fortress, for the sake of your name lead and guide me" (Ps. 31:3). With the hymn writer may we respond with this resolve: "Songs of praises, I will ever give to Thee."

Martin Luther King Jr. Day

~

Freedom cannot long survive unless it is based on moral
foundations.

—Author Unknown

Martin Luther King Jr., born on January 15, 1929, and assassinated on April 4, 1968, is generally acknowledged as the most
important leader of the struggle by African-Americans to achieve
full equality in America. King was not only a champion of equal
rights achieved through peaceful civil disobedience; he was also
a Baptist minister, an author, and a graduate of Boston University with a doctor of philosophy degree. In 1964, he was awarded
the Nobel Peace Prize.

The climax of the protest movement occurred on August 28,
1963, when two hundred thousand people marched on Washington, D.C., with the rallying cry, "Freedom Now!" The march-
ers gathered at the Lincoln Memorial. There, before the
monument of the man who had issued the Emancipation Proclamation one hundred years earlier, Martin Luther King Jr. gave
his famous "I Have a Dream" speech, telling how much remained
to be done before the freedom of African-Americans would truly
be complete. His vision for the future included these words:

When all of God's children, black men and white men, Jews and Gentiles, Protestants and Catholics, will be able to join hands and sing in the words of the old Negro spiritual, "Free at last! free at last! thank God Almighty, we are free at last!"

On April 3, 1968, King went to Memphis, Tennessee, to help organize a strike of the city's predominantly black sanitation workers. The next day, while he stood on a balcony of the hotel where he was staying, his life was suddenly ended by an assassin's bullet.

Though Martin Luther King's life was cut short before he saw the fulfillment of his dream, his forceful leadership, his vision, and his eloquent speeches set in motion needed reforms that now assure equal rights and opportunities for every individual, regardless of race.

Freedom is an indivisible word. If we want to enjoy it, and fight for it, we must be prepared to extend it to everyone, whether they are rich or poor, whether they agree with us or not, no matter what their race or the color of their skin.
—Wendell Willkie

Prayer

Give us, O Lord, a genuine love for people of all races and cultures, free of sinful prejudice and self-righteousness, and a passion to fervently pursue justice for all people. Help us to view every person as someone made in Your likeness and one for whom Christ died to redeem. Amen.

And let there be praise!

Be Thou my Vision, O Lord of my heart—
Nought be all else to me, save that
Thou art;
Thou my best thought, by day or
by night—
Waking or sleeping, Thy presence my light.

Be Thou my Wisdom, and Thou my
true Word—
I ever with Thee and Thou with me, Lord;
Thou my great Father, I Thy true son—
Thou in me dwelling, and I with
Thee one.

Riches I heed not, nor man's
empty praise—
Thou mine inheritance, now and always;
Thou and Thou only, first in my heart—
High King of heaven, my Treasure
Thou art.

High King of heaven, my victory won,
May I reach heaven's joys, O bright
heav'n's Sun!
Heart of my own heart, whatever befall,
Still be my Vision, O Ruler of all.

Be Thou My Vision

> Where there is no vision, the people perish: but he that keepeth
> the law, happy is he.
>
> —Proverbs 29:18 (KJV)

*T*his anonymous, eighth-century Irish hymn expresses in the quaint Celtic style the ageless need of man to live with a heavenly vision, experiencing God's guidance and presence throughout his earthly pilgrimage.

For Christians, "vision" is an awareness of Christ in all His fullness and enabling power, and the desire to follow Him and live Christlike lives. The clearer that vision becomes, the more Christ becomes "my best thought," "my wisdom," "my true Word," "mine inheritance," "my victory," "my treasure." No longer do we seek after riches or "man's empty praise."

Vision—the ability to see a possibility of accomplishing a difficult task—is always the predecessor of any endeavor well done. Our visionary attitude throughout life is generally the difference between mediocrity and success. One is reminded of the classic story of the two shoe salesmen who were sent to a primitive island to determine business potential. The first salesman wired back, "Coming home immediately. No one here wears shoes." The second man responded, "Send a boatload of shoes immediately. The possibilities for selling shoes here are unlimited!"

Mary Byrne's English prose translation of an ancient Irish poem first appeared in the journal *Erin*, volume 2, published in 1905. Later it was put into verse form by Eleanor H. Hull and published in her *Poem Book of the Gael,* 1912. The tune "Slane" is a traditional Irish air from Patrick W. Joyce's collection, *Old Irish Folk Music and Songs,* published in 1909. The tune was originally used with a secular text, "With My Love on the Road." Its first association with this hymn was in the *Irish Church Hymnal* of 1919.

Mary Elizabeth Byrne was educated at the University of Dublin and became a research worker and writer for the Board of Intermediate Education in that town. Her most important literary works were her contributions to the *Old and Mid-Irish Dictionary* and the *Dictionary of the Irish Language.*

Eleanor H. Hull was the founder and secretary of the Irish Text Society and president of the Irish Literary Society in London. She also authored several books on Irish history and literature.

Another anonymous writer penned these significant thoughts about the importance of having a vision for one's life:

> A vision without a task is a dream;
> A task without a vision is drudgery;
> A vision with a task is the hope of the world.

May we as believers be characterized as people with vision— "looking unto Jesus the author and finisher of our faith" (Heb. 12:2 KJV).

A charge to keep I have—
A God to glorify,
Who gave His Son my soul to save
And fit it for the sky.

To serve the present age,
My calling to fulfill—
O may it all my pow'rs engage
To do my Master's will!

Arm me with jealous care,
As in Thy sight to live;
And O Thy servant, Lord, prepare
A strict account to give!

Help me to watch and pray,
And on Thyself rely;
And let me ne'er my trust betray,
But press to realms on high.

A Charge to Keep I Have

> As a prisoner for the Lord, then, I urge you to live a life worthy of
> the calling you have received.
>
> —Ephesians 4:1

*C*harles Wesley is said to have been inspired to write the text for this hymn while reading Matthew Henry's commentary on the book of Leviticus. In his thoughts on Leviticus 8:35, Henry wrote: "We shall everyone of us have a charge to keep, an eternal God to glorify, an immortal soul to provide for, one generation to serve." The text first appeared in Wesley's *Short Hymns on Select Passages of Holy Scriptures,* volume 1, 1762. It was published under the title "Keep the Charge of the Lord, That Ye Die Not." It was one of sixteen hymns by Charles Wesley from the book of Leviticus. The text reflects something of the spiritual zeal of the Wesley brothers and their early Methodist followers.

The Methodist hymnody begun by John and Charles Wesley in the eighteenth century was one of the most powerful evangelizing influences in England. Both brothers believed strongly in the spiritual potential of music and congregational singing. They used their hymns to "arouse sinners, encourage saints, and to educate all in the mysteries of the Christian faith." The sixty-five hundred hymns written by Charles Wesley covered every phase of Christian experience and Methodist theology. In 1710, the Wesleys published a comprehensive hymnal that comprised the many hymns that had been used in their work of evangelism. Other well-known Charles Wesley hymns still in use today include "Christ the Lord Is Risen Today," "Jesus, Lover of My Soul," "Depth of Mercy," and "O for a Thousand Tongues."

The Wesleys often incurred opposition and persecution in their ministry for God. Sometimes, mob harassment was inflamed by the local Anglican clergymen, who would go from house to house charging that the Wesleys were preaching blasphemy against the established state church and thus should be run out of town. The early Methodist followers were also treated badly. Often they were physically mauled, their homes looted, and their businesses ruined.

Eighty years after the text was written, Lowell Mason, an American educator and musician, composed the tune, called "Boylston." Mason is often called the "father of American church and public school music." He is credited with composing or arranging approximately seven hundred hymn tunes, including such favorites as "Joy to the World," "Nearer My God to Thee," and "When I Survey the Wondrous Cross."

The task of being a Christian who worthily represents the Lord has never been, and will never be, an easy one. It demands our very best—the total commitment of our lives.

> Awake, my soul! Stretch every nerve, and press with vigor on;
> A heavenly race demands thy zeal, and an immortal crown.
> —Philip Doddridge

Valentine's Day

~

Live a life of love, just as Christ loved us.

—Ephesians 5:2

*T*his special day, the year's most romantic celebration, affords us the opportunity for expressing love and affection to friends, family, and lovers in a very personal way. In its noblest form, love is the gift of ourselves to someone we affectionately appreciate.

Love is not getting but giving; not a wild dream of pleasure, and a madness of desire—oh, no, love is not that—it is goodness, and honor, and peace and pure living.

—Henry Van Dyke

There are many conflicting stories about the origin of Valentine's Day. None of these various speculations can be fully substantiated, however. One of the most popular theories is that Valentine's Day replaced the pagan celebration known as the Feast of Lupercalia when the Christian religion began to be prominent in the Roman Empire. It is believed that a Roman physician named Valentine was especially helpful to the Christians during their time of persecution. His death is said to have occurred on February 14, 269, and two centuries later the pope set aside this date to perpetuate St. Valentine's memory. Gradually, the new Christian holiday became a time for sharing gifts and messages of affection, and St. Valentine emerged as the patron saint of lovers.

It's easy to talk sentimentally about love. It's much more difficult to apply it to needy people and situations. Scripture clearly teaches, however, that the proof of God's presence within our lives is the willingness to share His love with humanity. The earthly badge of our heavenly citizenship is our loving relationship with others.

> Love is silence—when your words would hurt.
> Love is patience—when your neighbor's curt.
> Love is deafness—when a scandal flows.
> Love is thoughtfulness—for others' woes.
> Love is promptness—when stern duty calls.
> Love is courage—when misfortune falls.

An old American folk hymn expresses our love for the Lord with these words:

> I love Thee, I love Thee and that Thou dost know;
> But how much I love Thee my actions will show.

Prayer

Dear God, may we be effective witnesses to family, friends, and acquaintances so that we are truly Your disciples by the love that we share with one another. Amen.

And let there be praise!

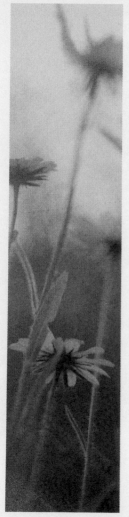

O Love that wilt not let me go,
I rest my weary soul in Thee;
I give Thee back the life I owe,
That in Thine ocean depths its flow
May richer, fuller be.

O Light that foll'west all my way,
I yield my flick'ring torch to Thee;
My heart restores its borrowed ray,
That in Thy sunshine's blaze its day
May brighter, fairer be.

O Joy that seekest me thru pain,
I cannot close my heart to Thee;
I trace the rainbow thru the rain,
And feel the promise is not vain
That morn shall tearless be.

O Cross that liftest up my head,
I dare not ask to fly from Thee;
I lay in dust life's glory dead,
And from the ground there blossoms red
Life that shall endless be.

O Love That Wilt
Not Let Me Go

> I have loved you with an everlasting love;
> I have drawn you with loving-kindness.
>
> —Jeremiah 31:3

O Love That Wilt Not Let Me Go" has long been regarded as one of the church's finest hymns on the theme of God's eternal love. The writing of this thoughtful text is even more remarkable when you consider that it was authored by someone who was totally blind and who described the writing as the "fruit of much mental suffering."

George Matheson had only partial vision as a young boy in Glasgow, Scotland. After he entered Glasgow University, his sight failed rapidly, and he became totally blind at the age of eighteen. Yet young Matheson never allowed his affliction to cause bitterness or resentment in his life. "My blindness has only deepened my dependency on the Lord," he often said. George Matheson went on to become one of Scotland's outstanding preachers, greatly esteemed wherever he ministered. Matheson's presentation in the pulpit was so vivid and attractive that visitors who heard him often left the church services completely unaware of his blindness.

Many conjectures have been made regarding the mental distress that prompted Matheson to write the text of this hymn in 1882. It is generally believed that it was the lingering memory of being rejected by his fiancée just before their scheduled marriage. Upon learning of Matheson's impending total blindness, the young lady reportedly responded, "I do not wish to be the wife of a blind preacher." George Matheson remained a bachelor for the rest of his life.

The music was composed one year later by a prominent Scotch organist, Albert L. Peace, who was asked by the Scottish Hymnal Committee to write a tune especially for Matheson's text. Mr. Peace left this account: "After reading the text carefully, I wrote the music straight off, and may say that the ink of the first note was hardly dry when I had finished the tune."

The four key words of this hymn are *love, light, joy,* and *cross.* These words have been described as the characteristics of any believer whose life is totally committed to the will of God. How thankful we should be that, regardless of the circumstances that come into our lives, we are related to a God who is from everlasting to everlasting and whose mercy and love for us are eternal. May this awareness stir our own lives to reflect and share God's love with others more fully each day.

> Who shall separate us from the love of Christ? Shall trouble or hardship . . . or danger or sword? . . . No, in all these things we are more than conquerors through him who loved us.
> —Romans 8:35, 37

Blest be the tie that binds
Our hearts in Christian love!
The fellowship of kindred minds
Is like to that above.

Before our Father's throne
We pour our ardent prayers;
Our fears, our hopes, our aims are one,
Our comforts and our cares.

We share our mutual woes,
Our mutual burdens bear;
And often for each other flows
The sympathizing tear.

When we asunder part
It gives us inward pain;
But we shall still be joined in heart,
And hope to meet again.

Blest Be the
Tie That Binds

Whoever loves his brother lives in the light, and there is nothing
in him to make him stumble.

—1 John 2:10

One of the blessings of the Christian life is the fellowship we
enjoy with other believers. Especially in times when deep sorrow
or difficulty enters our lives, the prayerful concern of fellow Christians is an undergirding comfort for such an hour.

"Blest Be the Tie That Binds" was born out of a deep spiritual
bond that existed between an English pastor of the eighteenth
century and his faithful parishioners. John Fawcett, born of poor
parents in Yorkshire, England, in 1740, was converted to Christ
at the age of sixteen through the forceful preaching of evangelist
George Whitefield. At the age of twenty-six, Fawcett was ordained
as a Baptist minister and accepted his first call to pastor a small
and impoverished congregation at Wainsgate in northern England. Wainsgate was not even a village; it was merely a strag-
gling group of poor houses at the top of a barren hill. The people
were farmers or poor shepherds, an uncouth lot, unable to read
or write, and cursed with wild tempers. The established Anglican Church had never touched their lives; only the humble Bap-
tists had earlier sent an itinerant preacher there, and he had made
a good beginning. Now they wanted young Fawcett to come and
minister to them.

He accepted the call, and with his new bride, Mary, arrived in Wainsgate. There was no parsonage awaiting them, and for quite some time they had to board around with their people. The salary was the equivalent of five or six dollars per month. But the Fawcetts' simple goodness and their devotion to everyone's welfare soon won the love of all. The congregation grew so rapidly that a new church addition had to be erected.

After seven years of devoted service under meager circumstances, John Fawcett received a call to the large and influential Carter's Lane Baptist Church in London. After the wagons were loaded for the move, the Fawcetts met their tearful parishioners for a final farewell. "John, I cannot bear to leave," whispered Mary. "Nor can I either," responded the saddened pastor. Then he announced, "We shall remain here with our people!"

The order was given to unload the wagons. On the following Sunday, John Fawcett preached from Luke 12:15: "A man's life consists not in the things he possesses." He closed his sermon by reading a new poem he had written, titled "Brotherly Love," which later became the beloved hymn "Blest Be the Tie That Binds."

John and Mary Fawcett continued their faithful ministry to the humble people of Wainsgate for a total of fifty-four years, until a paralytic stroke caused John's death on July 25, 1817, at the age of seventy-seven. Fawcett's salary was estimated to be never more than the equivalent of $200 a year, despite his growing reputation as an outstanding evangelical preacher, scholar, and writer. In recognition of his ministry and many accomplishments, including the establishment of a training school for young dissenting preachers, Brown University in Rhode Island conferred the doctor of divinity degree upon John Fawcett six years before his death.

> A loving relationship with fellow believers is a foretaste of heaven.
>
> —J. Fawcett

> The fellowship of kindred minds is like to that above.
>
> —J. Fawcett

Presidents' Day

~

Men must be governed by God or they will be ruled by tyrants.
—William Penn

In you our fathers put their trust; they trusted and you delivered them.
—Psalm 22:4

Until the 1970s, separate holidays were designated to honor two great leaders of the past, George Washington, our country's first president, and Abraham Lincoln, the sixteenth president of the United States. After the passing of the Monday Holiday Law in 1971, Washington's birthday (February 22) and Lincoln's birthday (February 12) are now jointly observed annually as a legal holiday on the third Monday in February. Gradually, this observance has evolved into a general celebration honoring all of the American presidents.

George Washington (1732–1799) is no doubt the most honored man our country has ever produced. He was commander in chief of the Continental Army. His persistence and bravery were crucial factors in the colonists' victory over the British forces. He then served as our first president from 1789–1797, and our nation's capital was named in his honor. Thomas Jefferson paid George Washington this tribute:

He was indeed in every sense of the word—a wise, a good, and a great man.

Abraham Lincoln (born 1809; assassinated on April 15, 1865, at the age of fifty-six) has been loved by the American people with a devotion never before or since given to any president. He is called the "Great Emancipator" for freeing the African-American race from slavery. In 1909, Congress passed a bill proposing the erection of a Lincoln memorial in our nation's capital. The monument, dedicated in May 1922, is one of the most visited spots in Washington, D.C.

One of the important freedoms in our land is the right to vote for the national, state, and local leaders we believe God destines to be in office. Our Constitution contains two amendments, Article XV and Article XIX, guaranteeing voting rights to every American citizen regardless of race or gender.

Prayer

Dear God, we thank You for the memory of our great leaders of the past. Continue to guide us as we exercise the dearly won freedom of choosing our present and future leaders. May this privilege neither be ignored unthinkingly nor taken lightly. Help those who are elected to public office to realize that their real mandate is from You. Together may we be known as a people who truly seek after righteousness. Amen.

And let there be praise!

God of our fathers, whose almighty hand
Leads forth in beauty all the starry band
Of shining worlds in splendor thru
the skies,
Our grateful songs before Thy
throne arise.

Thy love divine hath led us in the past,
In this free land by Thee our lot is cast;
Be Thou our ruler, guardian, guide,
and stay,
Thy word our law, Thy paths our
chosen way.

From war's alarms, from deadly
pestilence,
Be Thy strong arm our eversure defense;
Thy true religion in our hearts increase,
Thy bounteous goodness nourish us
in peace.

Refresh Thy people on their toilsome way,
Lead us from night to neverending day;
Fill all our lives with love and
grace divine,
And glory, laud, and praise be ever Thine!

God of Our Fathers

Give to Caesar what is Caesar's, and to God what is God's.
—Matthew 22:21

After what I owe to God, nothing should be more dear or more
sacred to me than the love and respect I owe my country.
—Jacques Auguste de Thou

No national holiday would be complete without a parade down
Main Street, the band playing a Sousa march, the Stars and Stripes
waving proudly in the breeze, and the crowd singing patriotic
songs. "God of Our Fathers" is a national hymn that has become
increasingly popular since Daniel Crane Roberts, an American
Episcopal minister, wrote it in 1876.

In that year, every city, town, and village in America was preparing to celebrate the one hundredth anniversary of the signing
of the Declaration of Independence. In Philadelphia, where the
Declaration was signed, the Centennial Exposition became the
largest fair ever held in America at that time. As the citizens of
the small village of Brandon, Vermont, were preparing for the
celebration, the rector of the small Episcopal church in that community decided to write a new patriotic hymn for the occasion.

Roberts was thirty-five years old when he wrote the text for
the now-familiar hymn. The parishioners of Brandon's St. Thomas Episcopal Church sang the hymn for the first time during
their worship service on July 4, 1876.

Later, at the time of the actual National Centennial celebration in New York City, Roberts's text was chosen as the official hymn for the event. Interestingly, however, the text was sung to the music of the old Russian national anthem. Perhaps because of this, the new hymn was slow in gaining acceptance.

After Roberts moved to Concord, New Hampshire, to become vicar of the historic St. Paul's Episcopal Church, he submitted his text anonymously to the committee responsible for revising the Episcopal hymnal, and the hymn was included in their 1892 edition—but it was still wedded with the Russian tune.

Two years later, the hymnal committee commissioned George Wilson Warren, organist of the St. Thomas Episcopal Church in New York City, to compose an original tune for Daniel Roberts's text. This new tune, with its dramatic trumpet calls before each stanza, was the key that unlocked the growing appreciation of the hymn. "God of Our Fathers" first appeared with its new tune, now known as the "National Hymn," in 1894 in the official hymnal of the Episcopal church. Roberts's text has been used exclusively with this music to the present time.

Roberts's words remind us anew that the God who has so richly blessed our land in the past is the one still needed to be "our ruler, guardian, guide, and stay."

O God, our help in ages past,
Our hope for years to come,
Our shelter from the stormy blast,
And our eternal home!

Under the shadow of Thy throne
Still may we dwell secure;
Sufficient is Thine arm alone,
And our defense is sure.

Before the hills in order stood
Or earth received her frame,
From everlasting Thou art God,
To endless years the same.

Time, like an ever-rolling stream,
Bears all its sons away;
They fly, forgotten, as a dream
Dies at the opening day.

O God, our help in ages past,
Our hope for years to come,
Be Thou our guide while life shall last,
And our eternal home.

O God, Our Help in Ages Past

> Lord, you have been our dwelling place
> > throughout all generations.
> Before the mountains were born
> > or you brought forth the earth and the world,
> > from everlasting to everlasting you are God.
> > > —Psalm 90:1–2

$\mathcal{O}$ God, Our Help in Ages Past" is regarded by many Christians as the grandest expression of praise in the whole realm of hymnody. It was written by Isaac Watts, often called the "father of the English hymn."

Before Watts's time, there were no hymns in English as we know them today. The music of the church was strictly singing of the psalms. In the seventeenth century, it would have been considered an insult to God for someone to use His own words for a sacred song. Only the actual words that God had dictated in Scripture were counted worthy for His praise.

At an early age, Watts became deeply concerned about the deplorable state to which congregational singing had degenerated in most English-speaking churches. He often exclaimed: "The singing of God's praise is the part of worship nearest heaven, but its performance among us is the worst on earth." Watts proceeded to write new paraphrases of the psalms, intending to give them a New Testament interpretation and style. In 1719, he published an important hymnal titled *The Psalms of David Imitated in the Language of the New Testament*. Watts paraphrased the entire

Psalter, with the exception of twelve psalms that he felt were unsuited for Christian usage. In addition to "O God, Our Help in Ages Past," based on Psalm 90, several of his other well-known hymns from that hymnal include "Joy to the World" (Ps. 98), "Jesus Shall Reign" (Ps. 72), and "Before Jehovah's Awful Throne" (Ps. 100).

As time passed, Watts grew more convinced that writers should be free to express praise and devotion to God in their own words rather than being limited to the literal wording of Scripture. These hymns became known as "hymns of human composure" and included such favorites as "When I Survey the Wondrous Cross," "Am I a Soldier of the Cross?" and "I Sing the Mighty Power of God." In all, Watts wrote more than six hundred hymns during his lifetime.

Although Isaac Watts was small in stature and delicate in health, he was a scholarly genius in many different areas. His writings included essays on psychology, three volumes of sermons, numerous treatises on theology, a textbook on logic, and a variety of other works. Many of these writings had a profound influence upon the literary world of the eighteenth century.

A great hymn deserves majestic music. The "St. Anne" tune was composed by one of the finest English musicians of his day, William Croft. He dedicated the tune to the reigning monarch, Queen Anne.

After more than 250 years, Isaac Watts's hymn is still a timely reminder of God's faithfulness throughout the past and His sure promises for our future.

Mother's Day, Father's Day, Children's Day

~

Four things in any land must dwell,
If it endures and prospers well;
One is manhood true and good;
One is noble womanhood;
One is child life, clean and bright;
And one an altar kept alight.

—Author Unknown

Mother's Day

Show me the mothers of a people and I will show you the
nation.

—Billy Sunday

Mother's Day is one of the most widely celebrated holidays of
the year. It is observed annually on the second Sunday in May.
The week that culminates with Mother's Day is designated as
Christian Family Week.

Anna M. Jarvis promoted the idea for a special day for mothers after her own mother died in 1905. Julia Ward Howe, author
of the "Battle Hymn of the Republic," had earlier suggested the
day as a way of reuniting families divided by the Civil War. The
special day was officially recognized on May 9, 1914, when Presi-

dent Woodrow Wilson issued a proclamation setting aside the second Sunday in May for expressing our love and appreciation for the mothers of our country.

Father's Day

The glory of children are their fathers.

—Proverbs 17:6 (KJV)

Father's Day, observed on the third Sunday in June, was first suggested by Mrs. John Bruce Dodd in 1909 and celebrated one year later in her church in Spokane, Washington. In 1924, President Calvin Coolidge officially approved the observance of the day. In 1972, the day was established permanently when President Richard Nixon signed a congressional resolution placing Father's Day on the same continuing basis as Mother's Day.

The imprint of the parents remains forever in the life of a child.

—Author Unknown

Children's Day

Let the little children come to me, and do not hinder them,
for the kingdom of heaven belongs to such as these.

—Matthew 19:14

The second Sunday in June has long been recognized by many Protestant churches in the United States as Children's Day—a time when the importance of young people as the future leaders of society and the church is recognized and emphasized.

Another special influence in any family relationship is the role of the grandparents. A day for their recognition was established by a presidential proclamation signed on September 6, 1979. It is observed on the first Sunday after Labor Day.

The strength of any nation shows in the quality of its homes. "In love of home, the country has its rise," said Charles Dickens. During these unsettled times, let us reaffirm our vows with Joshua of old:

> But as for me and my household, we will serve the LORD.
> —Joshua 24:15

Prayer

Dear Lord, help me to realize and practice these basic truths:
That the beauty of the home is order;
That the blessing of the home is contentment;
That the glory of the home is hospitality;
That the crown of the home is godliness. Amen.
—Author Unknown

And let there be praise!

For the beauty of the earth,
For the glory of the skies,
For the love which from our birth
Over and around us lies:
Christ our God, to Thee we raise
This our hymn of grateful praise.

For the wonder of each hour
Of the day and of the night,
Hill and vale and tree and flow'r,
Sun and moon and stars of light:
Christ our God, to Thee we raise
This our hymn of grateful praise.

For the joy of human love,
Brother, sister, parent, child,
Friends on earth and friends above,
For all gentle thoughts and mild:
Christ our God, to Thee we raise
This our hymn of grateful praise.

For Thy Church that evermore
Lifteth holy hands above,
Off'ring up on ev'ry shore
Her pure sacrifice of love:
Christ our God, to Thee we raise
This our hymn of grateful praise.

For the Beauty
of the Earth

Whatever is true, whatever is noble, whatever is right, whatever
is pure, whatever is lovely, whatever is admirable—if anything is
excellent or praiseworthy—think about such things.

—Philippians 4:8

$\mathcal{F}$or the Beauty of the Earth" reminds us of many normal blessings of life that often we take for granted—the beauties of the
natural world, as well as the joys of friends, home, and church—
blessings that bring such enriching dimensions to our daily lives.
The hymn's author directs our "grateful praise" to God, the giver
of every good and perfect gift.

Not much is known about Folliott S. Pierpoint, the author of
this lovely text. He was born in the intriguing old town of Bath,
England, and was a lay member of the Anglican church. Even
today, Bath is a most interesting town, nestled in the hills, where
one can still view the large pools of natural mineral baths for
which the town was named. Following Pierpoint's graduation
from Cambridge University, he taught the classics for a time at
Somerset College before becoming an independent writer. Although he wrote seven volumes of poems, most of them based
on his love for nature, he is best remembered today for this one
beautiful hymn text.

The inspiration for the text is said to have come to the young
author one spring day as he was strolling about his native town

of Bath. He was entranced by the charming countryside and the winding Avon River in the distance. As his heart welled up with emotion, he expressed with his pen the feelings of gratitude that were within him. The text first appeared in 1864 in a collection of his poems. He titled the hymn text "The Sacrifice of Praise." An interesting verse not included in most hymnals gives thanks for God Himself, who has made all of the beauties and joys of life possible.

> For Thyself, best Gift Divine!
> To our race so freely given;
> For that great, great love of Thine,
> Peace on earth, and joy in heav'n,
> Lord of all, to Thee we raise
> This our hymn of grateful praise.

The tune name "Dix" comes from the association of this melody with William Dix's Christmas hymn, "As with Gladness Men of Old." Its composer, Conrad Kocher, was a prominent nineteenth-century German musician and reformer of church music.

"For the Beauty of the Earth" was first used for church Communion services. It has since become one of the favorite hymns for the Thanksgiving season, as well as for special family holidays when parents and children are honored. Like many of our timeless texts that are simply stated and easily understood, this hymn is a favorite with young and old alike.

I lift my heart to Thee, O God, in gratitude and praise
For all Thy blessings of the past, and those of future days—

For well I know if I shall live, Thy blessings still will flow
Across my soul in greater joy than I could ever know.

I thank Thee for my faithful friends, for sunshine and the rain,
And every blessing hid or seen, though some may come through
    pain.
O God, accept my thanks to Thee each time I come to pray,
And grant each day that I shall live will be a thankful day.

—Author Unknown

Happy the home when God is there
And love fills ev'ry breast,
When one their wish and one their prayer
And one their heav'nly rest.

Happy the home where Jesus' name
Is sweet to ev'ry ear,
Where children early lisp His fame
And parents hold Him dear.

Happy the home where prayer is heard
And praise is wont to rise,
Where parents love the sacred Word
And all its wisdom prize.

Lord, let us in our homes agree
This blessed peace to gain;
Unite our hearts in love to Thee,
And love to all will reign.

Happy the Home
When God Is There

He is happiest, be he king or peasant, who finds peace in his own home.

—Johann Wolfgang Goethe

If anyone loves me, he will obey my teaching. My Father will love him, and we will come to him and make our home with him.

—John 14:23

*T*he importance of a loving home life in childhood cannot be overemphasized. The character of a child and the direction of his life are strongly influenced by the home. As the years go by, one who has lived in a peaceful and loving environment has pleasant memories that help in coping with the daily struggles and frustrations. How sad it is, however, to hear of many homes in our society today in which there is turbulence, conflict, and even abuse. In such homes there is no real love or happiness. We are reminded in this lovely hymn that only the home where God is honored is a truly joyful one.

It is surprising that our hymnals do not include more hymns about the home and the family. "Happy the Home When God Is There" is the one that appears most often. It was first published in 1846 in *Selection of Hymns and Poetry for Use of Infant and Juvenile Schools and Families*.

Henry Ware Jr. was well acquainted with the hymn's subject

of home life, because he grew up as one of a family of eight children, and he himself became the father of nine. He was educated at Harvard University, where his father, Dr. Henry Ware Sr., was a professor in the divinity school. Young Henry taught briefly in the Exeter Academy, but after he was ordained, he accepted the pastorate of the Second Unitarian Church in Boston, Massachusetts. His assistant in the church for a time was the noted American poet, Ralph Waldo Emerson.

In his later years, Pastor Ware served as a professor at the Cambridge Theological School. He was also the editor of a publication titled *The Christian Disciple,* later renamed *The Christian Examiner.* Even with such a demanding career and the pressures of raising a large family, Ware completed four volumes of writing, including several hymns. His text about the home where God is exalted is his best-known work.

Before writing this fine hymn, Pastor Ware must certainly have observed and counseled many families in his congregation. Consequently, he advises that the key to a truly happy home is the presence of God. He stresses the necessity of spiritual guidance through closeness to Christ, frequency of prayer and praise, and knowledge of the Bible.

John B. Dykes, a highly regarded English composer, wrote the music for this hymn. After a musical education at Cambridge University, Dykes composed approximately three hundred hymn tunes and received an honorary doctorate in music from Durham University. Some of his enduring compositions are "Jesus, the Very Thought of Thee," "Lead, Kindly Light," and "Holy, Holy, Holy."

In the quiet home life, showing love's bright way,
More and more like Jesus living every day,
We may guide a dear one to the heavenward way
By the things we practice, by the words we say.

—Author Unknown

Reflect on ways that the quality of our Christian homes could be improved. Consider seriously this question: Does God really have His rightful place as the foundation of my home?

Love the LORD your God with all your heart and with all your soul and with all your strength. These commandments that I give to you today are to be upon your hearts. Impress them on your children.

—Deuteronomy 6:5–7

Memorial Day

~

Lives of brave men all remind us
We can make our lives sublime,
And, departing, leave behind us
Footprints on the sands of time.
—Henry Wadsworth Longfellow

The boundary lines have fallen for me [us] in pleasant places;
surely I [we] have a delightful inheritance.

—Psalm 16:6

*T*he earliest observance of this day occurred on May 5, 1866, shortly after the close of the Civil War. The original purpose was to honor the war dead from both the North and South as a means of healing the wounds of our country's split. The day was originally called Decoration Day. As time passed and other wars were fought, the day commemorated the lives of all who had died in any of our military conflicts. Gradually the day also became the occasion to honor and decorate the grave sites of family and friends.

Throughout our land, Memorial Day has become associated with exciting parades featuring various military groups. At Arlington National Cemetery, the day is always marked with an impressive service in which the sacrifices and deeds of our war heroes are remembered. Around the world, Memorial Day is also observed wherever American servicemen are buried.

> A noble life, crowned with heroic death, rises above and outlives the pride and pomp and glory of the mightiest empire on the earth.
>
> —President James Garfield

For Christians, Memorial Day is also an appropriate time to remember fellow church members who were called to their heavenly home during the past year. It is also a good time to offer thanks for the individuals who have especially influenced our lives—directing us to God, tutoring us in truth, and modeling the virtues of the Christian life.

> God save America! 'Mid all her splendors,
> Save her from pride and from luxury;
> Throne in her heart the unseen and eternal;
> Right be her might and the truth make her free!
>
> —John Ellerton

Prayer

Thank You, God, for this day, which encourages us to reflect on the host of individuals who through the centuries have contributed so much to our nation's freedom. We are also thankful for the memories of precious loved ones and friends who are now enjoying Your eternal presence. For these blessings we are grateful.

And let there be praise!

Mine eyes have seen the glory
of the coming of the Lord,
He is trampling out the vintage
where the grapes of wrath are stored;
He hath loosed the fateful lightning
of His terrible swift sword—
His truth is marching on.

REFRAIN:
Glory! glory, hallelujah!
Glory! glory, hallelujah!
Glory! glory, hallelujah!
His truth is marching on.

I have seen Him in the watchfires
of a hundred circling camps,
They have builded Him an altar
in the evening dews and damps;
I can read His righteous sentence
by the dim and flaring lamps—
His day is marching on.

In the beauty of the lilies
Christ was born across the sea,
With a glory in His bosom
that transfigures you and me;
As He died to make men holy,
let us die to make men free,
While God is marching on.

Battle Hymn of
the Republic

Some trust in chariots and some in horses,
but we trust in the name of the LORD our God.
—Psalm 20:7

$\mathcal{T}$he familiar patriotic hymn, "Battle Hymn of the Republic," was written by a remarkable lady named Julia Ward Howe during the early years of the Civil War.

Mrs. Howe and her husband had recently moved from Boston to Washington, D.C., where he was involved in medical service for the government. Julia became deeply anguished as she noted the growing angry mood of the nation and its frenzied preparation for the tragic conflict between our own people. Day after day, Mrs. Howe watched the troops marching off to war. She heard them singing the strains of "John Brown's Body," named for an abolitionist who had been hanged for his efforts to have the slaves freed.

One day, a parade of soldiers who were singing this catchy tune passed by Mrs. Howe's home. Her former pastor, the Reverend James Freeman Clarke of Boston, who was visiting her, said in disgust, "Julia, why don't you write some decent words for that tune?" "That I will!" was her immediate reply.

The new words came to her that same night. "I awoke in the grey of the morning, and as I lay waiting for dawn, the long lines of the desired poem began to entwine themselves in my mind, and I said to myself 'I must get up and write these verses down lest I fall asleep and forget them.' So I sprang out of bed and in the dimness found an old stump of a pen which I remembered using the day before. I scrawled the verses almost without looking at the paper."

Soon the entire nation was united in singing these new words: "Glory! glory hallelujah! His truth is marching on," rather than the many derisive phrases that had been coined for "John Brown's Body." Mrs. Howe's text, written in response to a challenge to make better words for an existing Southern camp meeting tune, was destined for immortality.

On one occasion at a large patriotic rally, President Lincoln heard the hymn sung. As the audience responded with loud applause, the president, with tears in his eyes, cried out, "Sing it again!" And again it was sung with great enthusiasm. The "Battle Hymn of the Republic" became accepted as one of our finest national hymns, and its original purpose as a battle song for the North was soon forgotten.

After the war, Julia Ward Howe continued working for causes of human rights until her death in 1910 at the age of ninety-one. She was also known for other publications, including three volumes of poetry. In addition, this remarkable woman was the mother of four children, all of whom distinguished themselves in the fields of science and literature.

Blessed is the nation whose God is the Lord.

—Psalm 33:12

Praise the LORD, all you nations; extol him, all you peoples. For great is his love toward us, and the faithfulness of the LORD endures forever.

—Psalm 117:1–2

My country, 'tis of thee,
Sweet land of liberty,
Of thee I sing:
Land where my fathers died,
Land of the pilgrims' pride,
From ev'ry mountain side
Let freedom ring!

My native country, thee,
Land of the noble free,
Thy name I love:
I love thy rocks and rills,
Thy woods and templed hills;
My heart with rapture thrills
Like that above.

Let music swell the breeze,
And ring from all the trees
Sweet freedom's song:
Let mortal tongues awake,
Let all that breathe partake;
Let rocks their silence break,
The sound prolong.

Our fathers' God, to Thee,
Author of liberty,
To Thee we sing:
Long may our land be bright
With freedom's holy light;
Protect us by Thy might,
Great God, our King!

My Country, 'Tis of Thee

Be still, and know that I am God;
I will be exalted among the nations,
I will be exalted in the earth.

—Psalm 46:10

Samuel Francis Smith, author of "My Country, 'Tis of Thee," was one of the outstanding Baptist preachers and patriots of the nineteenth century. At an early age, Smith's unusual scholastic ability became evident. He enrolled at Harvard University when he was seventeen, and later prepared for the ministry at Andover Seminary. After his ordination as a Baptist minister, Smith served several prominent churches, including the historic First Baptist Church in Newton, Massachusetts. During these years he authored several important books, compiled a Baptist hymnal, and wrote 150 hymn texts, including the familiar missionary hymn, "The Morning Light Is Breaking." Later in life he became secretary of the Baptist Missionary Union and spent considerable time visiting various foreign fields. Samuel Smith was also recognized as an accomplished linguist in fifteen different languages, and he began studying Russian at the age of eighty-six, just one year before his death.

One February day in 1831, while still in seminary, Smith met his close friend, Lowell Mason, a noted music educator, church musician, and the choirmaster at Park Street Church of Boston. Mason had recently received a book of songs extolling the virtues of Germany and asking God's continued blessing upon that

77

nation. He remarked that it was a shame the United States didn't have a similar national hymn that would enable the American people to direct praise and thanks to God for this great land.

Young Samuel Smith agreed to translate the German songs for Dr. Mason. Smith recalled, "As I worked on these translations, however, I felt the impulse to write a patriotic song of my own, adapted to the familiar tune long associated with the English words of 'God Save the King.' Picking up a piece of scrap paper which lay near by, I wrote at once—probably within thirty minutes—the hymn 'America' as it is now known everywhere. The whole hymn stands today as it first appeared on that bit of scrap paper."

Samuel Smith's song was introduced at an outdoor Independence Day celebration on the next July 4. Lowell Mason's two-hundred-voice children's choir suddenly rose and began to sing with loud, clear voices, "My country, 'tis of thee, Sweet land of liberty, . . ." The large crowd joined the children in singing the new patriotic song, and soon the entire nation adopted it.

An eminent leader of that era once paid this tribute to the hymn:

Strong in simplicity and deep in its trust in God, children and philosophers can repeat the hymn together. Every crisis will hear it above the storm.

As Christian citizens of this great nation, may we be known as people who always speak well of our beloved land, extolling its virtues, and grateful to God for His many blessings.

Give thanks to the LORD, call on his name;
make known among the nations what he has done,
and proclaim that his name is exalted.

—Isaiah 12:4

Independence Day

~

> It ought to be commemorated as the day of deliverance, by solemn
> acts of devotion to God Almighty. It ought to be solemnized with
> pomp and parade . . . bonfires and illuminations from one end of
> the continent to the other, from this time forward forevermore.
> —John Adams (1776)

*I*ndependence Day is the most important patriotic holiday of
the American year. It is an annual celebration of the signing of
the Declaration of Independence on July 4, 1776—the birth of
our nation. Thomas Jefferson drafted this important document
at the first Continental Congress held in Philadelphia on September 5, 1774, and it was finally ratified on July 4, 1776.

> We hold these truths to be self-evident that all men are cre-
> ated equal, that they are endowed by their Creator with cer-
> tain inalienable rights. . . . That among these are life, liberty
> and the pursuit of happiness.

This statement was signed by the fifty-six members of the
Continental Congress at great risk to their lives. It was no doubt
a most inspiring and solemn occasion when these men stepped
forward to place their signatures with this statement:

And for the support of this Declaration, with a firm reliance
on the protection of Divine Providence, we mutually pledge
to each other our lives, our fortunes, and our honor.

In 1794, Congress approved a national flag with fifteen stars
and fifteen stripes. It served from 1795 to 1818 and is the flag
that inspired Francis Scott Key to write our national anthem. On
August 3, 1949, Congress passed a resolution signed by President Harry S. Truman officially designating June 14 as Flag Day.

We do honor to the stars and stripes as the emblem of our
country and the symbol of all that our patriotism means. . . .
A yearly contemplation of our flag strengthens and purifies
the national conscience.

—President Calvin Coolidge

Thou, too sail on, O Ship of State!
Sail on, O Union, strong and great!
Humanity with all its fears,
With all the hopes of future years
Is hanging breathless on thy fate.
We know what Master laid thy keel—
Our hearts, our hopes, are all with thee,
Our hearts, our hopes, our prayers, our tears,
Our faith triumphant o'er our fears,
Are all with thee—are all with thee.

—Henry Wadsworth Longfellow

These Colors Don't Run

In the bright morning light like a thief in the night
The terrors rained down on the city;
Our horizons have changed but our strength it remains,
And to evil we'll show no pity.

Now our children will grow and we'll teach them to know
Of the spirit that held us together;
For our values are strong and we know right from wrong,
And this world we will change for the better.

Many colors are we in the land of the free,
And we live brave and true under red, white and blue;
A new day has begun—we're united as one,
This war will be won— "These colors don't run!"

—Buddy King
All rights reserved, 2001
Used by permission

Prayer

Dear God, thank You for this special day when we celebrate the birth of our great nation. We are grateful for the memory of those early leaders who acknowledged You as man's Creator and signed the Declaration of Independence at the risk of their own lives. May their example of courage and conviction continue to inspire our people to build upon the spiritual principles of this firm foundation. Amen.

And let there be praise!

O say, can you see,
by the dawn's early light,
What so proudly we hailed
at the twilight's last gleaming,
Whose broad stripes and bright stars,
thru the perilous fight,
O'er the ramparts we watched,
were so gallantly streaming?
And the rockets' red glare,
the bombs bursting in air,
Gave proof thru the night
that our flag was still there.
O say, does that star-spangled
banner yet wave
O'er the land of the free
and the home of the brave?

O thus be it ever,
when free men shall stand
Between their loved homes
and the war's desolation!
Blest with vict'ry and peace,
may the heav'n-rescued land
Praise the Pow'r that hath made
and preserved us a nation!
Then conquer we must,
when our cause it is just;
And this be our motto:
"In God is our trust!"
And the star-spangled banner
in triumph shall wave
O'er the land of the free
and the home of the brave!

The Star-Spangled Banner

Submit yourselves for the Lord's sake to every authority insti-
tuted among men: whether to the king, as the supreme authority,
or to governors, who are sent by him to punish those who do
wrong and to commend those who do right.

—1 Peter 2:13–14

*F*rancis Scott Key, author of our national anthem, was the son of a distinguished Revolutionary War officer. He served as the district attorney of Georgetown, District of Columbia, for three terms. Throughout his life, Francis was known as a fine Christian gentleman and an active lay leader in the Protestant Episcopal church.

During the War of 1812 against England, Francis Scott Key was authorized by President James Madison to visit the British fleet located near the mouth of the Potomac to negotiate the release of a physician friend, Dr. Beanes, who had been taken prisoner by the invaders. The British admiral finally granted the American's request, but because the British ships had planned an attack on Fort McHenry, which guarded the harbor of Baltimore, Key and his party were detained all night aboard the truce boat on which they had come.

September 13, 1813, was a night of unforgettable anxiety for Key and his party as the fierce bombardment continued during the hours of darkness. As long as the shore fortification replied to the attack, Key and his friends were certain that all was still going well. Toward morning, however, the firing from the shore seemed to cease, causing the American delegation great dismay. Key paced the deck until the first rays of dawn revealed that the "flag was still there"—assurance that America was still free. Inspired by this experience, Francis began to write his poem hastily on the back of an envelope. That evening, upon being released, he completed the work in his home.

Approximately one month later, Key's poem was published in sheet music form by Joseph Carr and was set to a tune known as "Anacron in Heaven," an old hunting melody. The song was titled "The Defense of Fort McHenry" and enjoyed great popularity. Soon it was retitled "The Star-Spangled Banner." Because of the song, the country itself would ever after be known as the "land of the free and the home of the brave."

The last stanza, though seldom sung, reflects something of Francis Scott Key's spiritual convictions. He hoped that his beloved nation would always be characterized as praising "the Pow'r that hath made and preserved us a nation," and that our motto would always be "In God is our trust."

In honor of this Christian patriot and author of our national anthem, a fine statue was erected and can still be seen in the city of Baltimore. Despite the early enthusiastic acceptance of this patriotic hymn, it was not officially adopted and declared by Congress to be our national anthem until March 3, 1931.

During these days of turmoil and tension, when the many terrorists throughout the world are bent on our nation's destruction, may the musical question from our national anthem be a continuing challenge and concern for each of us:

O say, does that star-spangled banner yet wave
O'er the land of the free and the home of the brave?

—Francis Scott Key

God is our refuge and strength, an ever-present help in trouble.
Therefore we will not fear . . .

—Psalm 46:1–2

O beautiful for spacious skies,
For amber waves of grain,
For purple mountain majesties
Above the fruited plain!
America! America!
God shed His grace on thee,
And crown thy good with brotherhood
From sea to shining sea.

O beautiful for heroes proved
In liberating strife,
Who more than self their country loved
And mercy more than life!
America! America!
May God thy gold refine,
Till all success be nobleness,
And ev'ry gain divine.

O beautiful for patriot dream
That sees, beyond the years,
Thine alabaster cities gleam—
Undimmed by human tears!
America! America!
God shed His grace on thee,
And crown thy good with brotherhood
From sea to shining sea.

America the Beautiful

The fruit of righteousness will be peace; the effect of righteousness will be quietness and confidence forever.

—Isaiah 32:17

To have put the expression of the highest and deepest patriotism
into the mouths of a hundred million Americans is a monument so
noble and so enduring that it seems as if no poet could possibly
ask or expect anything more complete.

The above tribute was given in a memorial service for Katharine
Lee Bates at the time of her death in 1929. Her poem, "America
the Beautiful," had already become one of our country's favorite
patriotic hymns.

Katharine Bates was born in Falmouth, Massachusetts, in 1859.
She devoted nearly half a century of her life to Wellesley College.
She arrived there as a seventeen-year-old student and died there
as a professor of English literature at the age of seventy. She became widely acclaimed as a literary specialist and was honored
with doctorate degrees from several universities.

"America the Beautiful" was never intended to become a hymn
text. Bates's first desire was to write a poem commemorating the
four hundredth anniversary of Columbus's discovery of America.
A short time later, while she was visiting and teaching during the
summer months in the state of Colorado and had the opportunity to visit the summit of Pike's Peak, the inspiration for the
opening lines of the text formed themselves in her mind.

Still later in that same year of 1893, Miss Bates visited the World's Fair Columbian Exposition that ran for several years in Chicago. On the site of the exposition, magnificent buildings were erected. Thousands of people came from all over the world to marvel at the splendor and grandeur of such a spectacle. The expression "alabaster cities" was the result of that visit. "It was my desire," said Bates "to compare the unusual beauties of God's nature in this country with the distinctive spectacles created by man."

The hymn also reminds us forcibly of our noble heritage—the pilgrims as well as the liberating heroes. Miss Bates spoke often of the truth that unless we crown our good with brotherhood, of what lasting value are our spacious skies, our amber waves of grain, our mountain majesties, or our fruited plains? She would add, "We must match the greatness of our country with the goodness of personal godly living."

The hymn attained widespread popularity for the first time during the difficult days of World War I, when it did much to encourage patriotic pride and loyalty among the American people. "America the Beautiful" also enjoys the distinction of being the first song ever used in outer space. In 1960, as our communications satellite, Echo One, orbited high above the earth, it received and relayed to the United States this hymn.

> America! America!
> May God thy gold refine,
> Till all success be nobleness,
> And ev'ry gain divine.

Righteousness exalts a nation, but sin is a disgrace to any people.

—Proverbs 14:34

Labor Day

~

Be strong, all you people of the land, . . . and work. For I am with you.
—Haggai 2:4

No man needs sympathy because he has to work. . . . Far and away the best prize that life affords is the chance to work hard at work worth doing.

—Theodore Roosevelt

Labor is one of the great elements of society—the great substantial interest on which we all stand. Not feudal service . . . or the irksome drudgery of one race of mankind subjected, on account of their color, to another; but labor, intelligent, manly, independent, thinking and acting for itself, earning its own wages, accumulating those wages into capital, educating childhood, maintaining worship, claiming the right of elective franchise, and helping to uphold the great fabric of the state—that is American labor.

—Daniel Webster

*L*abor Day is a national holiday established to pay tribute each year to the many talents and efforts that have made America great. It was first promoted by Peter J. McGuire, president and founder of the United Brotherhood of Carpenters and Joiners of America. McGuire had a deep respect for his fellow workers and a passionate desire to improve their working conditions. On September 5, 1882, the first Labor Day observance took place in New York City. Soon the day grew in popularity across the land. On June 28, 1893, President Grover Cleveland signed the law designating the first Monday in September as a legal holiday for our nation's workers.

Industrial workers have been a major influence in the rise of our nation's power and strength. Unfortunately, workers have at times been shamefully exploited, often working for low wages under difficult and hazardous working conditions. Efforts to improve the workers' lot have produced a gradual improvement during the twentieth century and up to the present. During this time, vast numbers of the nation's workers have joined the powerful labor union movement in the struggle for greater recognition.

> We are not here to play, to dream, to drift,
> We have hard work to do, and loads to lift;
> Shun not the struggle, face it—
> 'Tis God's gift.
>
> —Maltbie D. Babcock

Prayer

Thank You, Lord, for the blessing of work. Whatever the task, may we do it heartily as to the Lord, recognizing it as a sacred trust. May our attitudes even while working be an effective witness for the gospel. With the apostle Paul we affirm: "To this end I labor, struggling with all his energy, which so powerfully works in me" (Col. 1:29). Amen.

And let there be praise!

Rise up, O Church of God!
Have done with lesser things;
Give heart and mind and soul
*   and strength*
To serve the King of kings.

Rise up, O Church of God!
His kingdom tarries long;
Bring in the day of brotherhood
And end the night of wrong.

Rise up, O sons of God!
The Church for you doth wait,
Her strength unequal to her task,
Rise up, and make her great!

Lift high the cross of Christ!
Tread where His feet have trod;
As foll'wers of the Son of Man,
Rise up, O Church of God!

Rise Up, O Church
[Men] of God!

All authority in heaven and on earth has been given to me. Therefore go and make disciples of all nations, baptizing them in the name of the Father and of the Son and of the Holy Spirit, and teaching them to obey everything I have commanded you. And surely I am with you always, to the very end of the age.

—Matthew 28:18–20

The church universal, the "called out" body of believers in Christ from every age, race, and culture, has been given a momentous task—to "make disciples of all nations." This imposing edict was given by the One who not only issued the mandate but who also promised His accompanying presence until the task is completed.

The local church, individual congregations of Christians who realize that they have been chosen of God to accomplish His earthly purposes, must also keep the church's mission clearly in mind.

The first description of a New Testament church is given in Acts 2:41–47. In this Scripture are recorded five basic church functions that are still valid guidelines for today.

1. The Local Church Worships Together. The early church remained true to the Lord in doctrine, fellowship, breaking of bread, praying, and praising (vv. 42, 46, 47).
2. The Local Church Evangelizes Together. Three thousand people responded to the preaching, were baptized and

added to the church. Others were added daily as they were saved (vv. 41, 47).

3. The Local Church Learns Biblical Truth Together. This is called Christian education (v. 42).
4. The Local Church Fellowships Together. They had all things in common and were strongly unified (vv. 44, 46).
5. The Local Church Reaches Out Together. This represents social concern. They shared their resources with those in need (v. 45).

In a time when many churches have neglected their spiritual mandates and have become involved with "lesser things," it is imperative for concerned believers to renew their commitment to God's desires for the local church.

The author of this call-to-action text, William Pierson Merrill, was a Presbyterian minister. He served churches in Philadelphia and Chicago, and he pastored the large Brick Presbyterian Church in New York City until his retirement in 1938. Pastor Merrill wrote "Rise Up, O Men of God!" especially for the brotherhood movement within Presbyterian churches in 1911. In more recent times, some hymnal editors have changed the original title to include the entire body of Christ.

"Rise Up, O Church [Men] of God" teaches an important lesson: The way to a Christian's individual happiness is to be employed in doing something of value, to be "done with lesser things," and to be totally involved in serving "the King of kings."

The world at its worst needs the church at its best.
—Author Unknown

Let us watch, let us pray, and labor 'till the Master comes.
—Fanny Crosby

Work, for the night is coming,
Work through the morning hours;
Work while the dew is sparkling,
Work 'mid springing flowers;
Work while the day grows brighter,
Under the glowing sun;
Work, for the night is coming,
When man's work is done.

Work, for the night is coming,
Work through the sunny noon;
Fill brightest hours with labor,
Rest comes sure and soon:
Give every flying minute
Something to keep in store;
Work, for the night is coming,
When man works no more.

Work, for the night is coming,
Under the sunset skies;
While their bright tints are glowing,
Work, for daylight flies;
Work, till the last beam fadeth,
Fadeth to shine no more;
Work, while the night is dark'ning,
When man's work is o'er.

Work, for the Night Is Coming

As long as it is day, we must do the work of him who sent me.
Night is coming, when no one can work.

—John 9:4

Do not pray for easy lives; pray to be stronger men (people)! Do
not pray for tasks equal to your powers. Pray for powers equal to
your tasks. Then the doing of your work shall be no miracle, but
you shall be a miracle.

—Phillips Brooks

This hymn text, which emphasizes the diligence of working because of the urgency of the hour, is based on the challenging
words of Jesus: "Night is coming, when no one can work." Even
though for Christians every occupation is sacred when it is done
for God's glory, our primary concern in life is the work of the
gospel.

Use me, God, in Thy great harvest field,
Which stretcheth far and wide like a wide sea;
The gatherers are so few; I fear the precious yield
Will suffer loss. Oh, find a place for me!

—Christina G. Rossetti

The text for "Work, for the Night Is Coming" was written by an eighteen-year-old girl named Annie Louise Walker. Miss Walker was born in England but lived several years with her family in Canada. It was there that she wrote the hymn text. The poem first appeared in a Canadian newspaper in 1854. Later, Annie Louise returned to England and worked as a governess. In 1883, she married Harry Coghill, a wealthy merchant, and remained in England until her death at the age of seventy-one. Mrs. Coghill eventually attained prominence as a poet and an author of six novels as well as a book of children's plays. She will be best remembered, however, as the author of a simply worded hymn text written when she was just a teenager.

Ten years later, Lowell Mason, the noted American educator and musician who is often referred to as "the father of church and public school music in the U.S., composed the tune for Mrs. Coghill's text. It first appeared in Mason's book, *The Song Garden,* published in 1864, one of a series of public school music books he edited.

John Wesley once gave this advice to his eighteenth-century followers: "Never be unemployed and never be triflingly employed." Worthy work is a law of life. It began in the Garden of Eden when God gave Adam meaningful work to do:

> The LORD God took the man and put him in the Garden of
> Eden to work it and take care of it.
>
> —Genesis 2:15

What counts in God's sight is not only the actual work we do, but also the attitude with which we do it. A positive, cheerful attitude while working provides an effective witness for the gospel. A willingness to share the rewards of our work by meeting the needs of others is also the mark of a devoted follower of Christ.

> Let him labour, working with his hands the thing which is good, that he may have to give to him that needeth.
> —Ephesians 4:28 (KJV)

Columbus Day

~

Those who go down to the sea in ships,
Who do business on great waters;
They have seen the works of the LORD,
And His wonders in the deep.

—Psalm 107:23–24 (NASB)

Christopher Columbus was born in Genoa, Italy, in 1451. At an early age he became enamored with a new idea that the world was round. It was his dream to prove his theory by finding a water route to the Orient by sailing west. After being refused aid for this venture by the King of Portugal and later by the English government, he reached an agreement with Ferdinand and Queen Isabella of Spain for this voyage to the unknown. Columbus was given the title "admiral of all the ocean seas." He set forth on August 3, 1492, with a ninety-man crew and three vessels, the flagship Santa Maria, the Pinta, and the Niña. For more than a month, the vessels sailed without sighting land. Finally, the lookout on the Pinta shouted, "Tierra! Tierra!" That same morning, Columbus and the crew went ashore on an island and named it San Salvador. Today we know this area as the Bahamas.

Columbus made three more voyages to the new world, including visits to Cuba, Puerto Rico, and Panama. His failure to find gold and substantial wealth in these places eventually caused the Spanish government to lose interest in further expeditions, and Christopher Columbus died in 1506 in relative obscurity.

Today Columbus is ranked among the world's great explorers for initiating the systematic exploration and colonization of the new Western world. One historian has said: "Columbus was the greatest educator that ever lived, for he emancipated humanity from the narrowness of its ignorance ... and taught the lesson that human destiny, like divine mercy, arches over the whole world."

The American celebration in 1892 of the four hundredth anniversary of Columbus's landing was the first real interest shown in having a national holiday named in his honor. The day was originally known as Discovery Day. In 1968, President Lyndon B. Johnson signed a law designating the second Monday in October as a federal holiday in honor of the explorer who linked the old and new worlds together.

Prayer

Dear God, thank You for Your abiding presence in our lives so that we can say with absolute confidence:

I do not fear tomorrow, for I have lived today;
And though my course was stormy, my Pilot knew the way.
I do not fear tomorrow, if the sails set east or west;
On sea or safe in harbor, in Him, secure, I rest. Amen.

—Phyllis Michael

And let there be praise!

Eternal Father, strong to save,
Whose arm hath bound the restless wave,
Who bidd'st the mighty ocean deep
Its own appointed limits keep:
O hear us when we cry to Thee
For those in peril on the sea.

O Christ, the Lord of hill and plain,
O'er which our traffic runs amain
By mountain pass or valley low:
Wherever, Lord, Thy brethren go,
Protect them by Thy guarding hand
From ev'ry peril on the land.

O Spirit, whom the Father sent
To spread abroad the firmament:
O Wind of heaven, by Thy might
Save all who dare the eagle's flight,
And keep them by Thy watchful care
From ev'ry peril in the air.

O Trinity of love and pow'r,
Our brethren shield in danger's hour;
From rock and tempest, fire and foe,
Protect them wheresoe'er they go:
Thus evermore shall rise to Thee
Glad praise from air and land and sea.

Eternal [Almighty]
Father, Strong to Save

For this God is our God for ever and ever;
he will be our guide even to the end.

—Psalm 48:14

*E*ternal Father, Strong to Save," or better known to many as the "Navy Hymn," has often been described as the most popular hymn for busy travelers. It was written in 1860 by William Whiting and has gone through numerous revisions up to the present day. The hymn text was so well thought of when it was written that it was included in the 1861 edition of the highly regarded Anglican church hymnal, *Hymns Ancient and Modern*. It was set to the tune of "Melita," which was especially composed for it by one of England's highly esteemed church musicians of the nineteenth century, John B. Dykes. The tune was named for the island now called Malta (called Melita in the King James Version), where the apostle Paul was shipwrecked, as recorded in Acts 28:1.

The present version of the hymn is taken from the 1937 edition of the *Missionary Service Book*. One of the editors, Robert Nelson Spencer, added the second and third stanzas to include a plea for God's protection for those who travel by land and air as well as those on the high seas.

Little is known about the author, William Whiting, except that he was an Anglican churchman and that he held the position of headmaster at the Winchester College Choristers School for thirty-five years. He wrote several other hymn texts that are no longer in use. The composer, John B. Dykes, was highly recognized for his many musical accomplishments, including more than three hundred hymn tunes, many of which are still being used. His tunes have been described as the finest examples of the Victorian style of sacred music.

"Eternal Father, Strong to Save" (listed in some hymnals as "Almighty Father, Strong to Save") has been widely used in naval and state ceremonial functions both in England and the United States. Many will recall its stirring effect by the navy and marine bands at President John F. Kennedy's funeral on November 24, 1963.

It should be noted that the first three stanzas of this hymn are each addressed to a different member of the Godhead: Verse 1—to the Father who created and controls the seas (Job 38:10–11); verse 2—to the Son who has power to control the elements of nature (Matt. 8:23–27); verse 3—to the Spirit, who at the creation of the world "moved upon the face of the waters" (Gen. 1:2 KJV). The fourth stanza petitions the entire Trinity for the protection of those in air, on land and sea, and asks that the travelers' glad response might be praise that evermore would "rise to Thee."

> Let them give thanks to the LORD for his unfailing love
> and his wonderful deeds for men.
> —Psalm 107:31

> In his heart a man plans his course,
> but the LORD determines his steps.
> —Proverbs 16:9

Jesus, Savior, pilot me
Over life's tempestuous sea:
Unknown waves before me roll,
Hiding rocks and treach'rous shoal;
Chart and compass come from Thee—
Jesus, Savior, pilot me!

As a mother stills her child,
Thou canst hush the ocean wild;
Boist'rous waves obey Thy will
When Thou say'st to them, "Be still!"
Wondrous Sov'reign of the sea,
Jesus, Savior, pilot me!

When at last I near the shore,
And the fearful breakers roar
'Twixt me and the peaceful rest—
Then, while leaning on Thy breast,
May I hear Thee say to me,
"Fear not—I will pilot thee!"

Jesus, Savior, Pilot Me

Thou wilt shew me the path of life: in thy presence is fulness of joy; at thy right hand there are pleasures for evermore.

—Psalm 16:11 (KJV)

The steps of a good man are ordered by the LORD: and he delighteth in his way.

—Psalm 37:23 (KJV)

*J*esus, Savior, Pilot Me" was written in 1871 by a Presbyterian minister and was intended especially for the seafaring men who used the New York harbor. Edward Hopper, pastor of the Church of Sea and Land, a small church in the harbor area, wrote the text for his many sailor parishioners. He used language they knew well, referring to charts, compasses, and the absolute need for a competent pilot to guide their crafts through the tempestuous seas. The theme of the text is based on the gospel account recorded in Matthew 8:23–27, where Jesus calmed the raging Galilee Sea. "Even the winds and the waves obey him!" responded the amazed disciples.

Hopper wrote the hymn anonymously, as he did all of his works, and for some time no one knew that the pastor of the sailors was also the author of the sailors' favorite hymn. This was typical of Edward Hopper's humble, gentle spirit in all that he did for God. The poem first appeared in *The Sailor's Magazine* in 1871. Although this is the only hymn that Pastor Hopper wrote that is still in common use, it can be said of him as it can be of many other hymn writers:

> Happy is the man who can produce one song which the world
> will keep on singing after its author shall have passed away.
> —Author Unknown

Since its publication, the "sailor's song" has reached far beyond its original audience. It is a hymn that has been especially helpful to young people who are sincerely concerned about knowing God's will for their future lives.

Of the original six stanzas, only three are used today. One of the omitted stanzas is an interesting reminder of a constant need for Christ even when there are no disturbing storms and life appears calm.

> Though the sea be smooth and bright,
> Sparkling with the stars of night,
> And my ship's path be ablaze
> With the light of halcyon [peaceful] days,
> Still I know my need of Thee;
> Jesus, Savior, pilot me!

In 1886, at the age of seventy, Edward Hopper's prayer expressed in the third stanza of his own hymn had its fulfillment. He was found sitting in his study chair writing a new poem on the subject of heaven. This tribute was paid to him at his funeral:

> Suddenly the gentle, affectionate spirit of Edward Hopper

entered the heavenly "port" as he had requested, safely piloted by that never-failing friend, Jesus, whose Divine voice was still whispering to him, "Fear not, I will pilot thee."

> O Lord, the pilot's part perform,
> And guide and guard me thro' the storm;
> Defend me from each threat'ning ill,
> Control the waves, say, "Peace, be still."
>
> —William Cowper

Veterans / Armed Services Day

~

> God grants liberty only to those who love it, and are always ready
> to guard and defend it.
>
> —Daniel Webster

On November 11, 1918, an armistice was reached between the
allies and the central powers of Europe, ending four years of fierce
fighting in World War I— "the war to end all wars." A day known
as Armistice Day was soon established to honor the many Americans who had died in the service of their country. The day was
first observed on November 11, 1919.

Following World War II and the Korean War, there was a growing movement in this country to incorporate the honored dead
of all the American wars into the annual observance. The day
was then known as Veterans Day. President Dwight D. Eisenhower
signed it into law on June 1, 1954.

On May 21, 1960, President Eisenhower made this important
announcement from the White House:

> It is America's hope and purpose to work continually toward
> the peaceful adjustment of international differences, and it is
> fitting that Armed Services Day should emphasize the fact that
> our strength is dedicated to keeping the peace.

Throughout the nation's history, our armed services personnel have been called upon to defend our nation in order to maintain peace. On this special day we pay tribute to all who have served or who are now serving in one of the branches of the armed services.

Important Dates and Events in the Defense of Our Country

- January 17:   Operation Desert Storm began in 1991.
- January 27:   Signing of the Vietnam Peace Accord in 1973.
- April 11:   Persian Gulf cease-fire in 1991.
- May 8:   Germany's unconditional surrender in 1945.
- June 6:   D day—Allied invasion of Europe in 1944.
- June 25:   Korean War began in 1950.
- August 14:   Japan surrendered, ending World War II in 1945.
- September 2:   VJ Day—Japan signed formal surrender in 1945.
- September 11:   Patriot Day—terrorist attacks on U.S. in 2001.
- November 11:   Signing of the World War I armistice in 1918.
- December 7:   Japan's attack on Pearl Harbor in 1941.

The price of freedom has always been costly. It involves consistent vigilance and often the sacrifice of life itself.

Once to every man and nation comes the moment to decide,
In the strife of truth and falsehood, for the good or evil side.

—James Russell Lowell

Prayer

God of our fathers, known of old—
Lord of our far-flung battle line;
Lord God of Hosts, be with us yet,
Lest we forget! Lest we forget!

—Rudyard Kipling

And let there be praise!

Soldiers of Christ, arise
And put your armor on,
Strong in the strength which
God supplies
Through His eternal Son;
Strong in the Lord of hosts,
And in His mighty pow'r,
Who in the strength of Jesus trusts
Is more than conqueror.

Stand then in His great might,
With all His strength endued,
And take, to arm you for the fight,
The panoply of God;
From strength to strength go on,
Wrestle and fight and pray;
Tread all the pow'rs of darkness down,
And win the well-fought day.

Leave no unguarded place,
No weakness of the soul;
Take every virtue, ev'ry grace,
And fortify the whole.
That having all things done,
And all your conflicts past,
Ye may o'ercome through Christ alone,
And stand complete at last.

Soldiers of Christ, Arise

> Finally, be strong in the Lord and in his mighty power. Put on
> the full armor of God so that you can take your stand against
> the devil's schemes.
>
> —Ephesians 6:10–11

*F*ollowers of Christ are also His soldiers—called to do battle
with the forces of Satan and evil. We are to be active, aggressive
warriors, not merely passive recipients enjoying our spiritual
blessings.

Scripture also teaches that our warfare is a defensive struggle
against the evil terrorists who would destroy our souls.

> For our struggle is not against flesh and blood, but against
> the rulers, against the authorities, against the powers of this
> dark world and against the spiritual forces of evil in the heav-
> enly realms.
>
> —Ephesians 6:12

God's soldiers must always be dressed in the whole armor of
God if they are to ward off the darts of the unseen enemy. That
armor includes six vital pieces:

1. *The belt of truth*—warriors with absolute integrity.
2. *The breastplate of righteousness*—warriors who glorify God
   with their good works.

3. *Sandals of peace*—warriors who are peacemakers as well as aggressive soldiers.
4. *Helmet of salvation*—warriors whose minds are stayed on God.
5. *Sword of the Spirit*—warriors whose only offensive weapon is the Word of God.

In addition to wearing the spiritual armor, Christian soldiers are to face every occasion with prayer. This includes prayerful concern for fellow believers who are also doing battle with the enemy.

> And pray in the Spirit on all occasions with all kinds of prayers and requests. With this in mind, be alert and always keep on praying for all the saints.
>
> —Ephesians 6:18

"Soldiers of Christ, Arise" has often been referred to as "the Christian's bugle blast," because of its strong call to arms. The text was written by Charles Wesley, author of more than sixty-five hundred hymns covering the entire spectrum of Christian experience and doctrine. This hymn text was first published in 1749 and was titled "The Whole Armor of God—Ephesians VI." It originally had sixteen stanzas of eight lines each. The present version uses stanzas one, two, and sixteen.

The tune, "Diademata," was composed by George J. Elvey, an English musician of unusual skill. He was the organist for forty-seven continuous years at St. George's Chapel, Windsor, the home church of England's royal family. The tune was originally composed for the hymn text "Crown Him with Many Crowns."

As devoted soldiers of Christ, may we reaffirm with one of the outstanding missionaries of the past:

> I will place no value on anything I have or may possess except in relation to the Kingdom of Christ.
>
> —David Livingstone

Lead on, O King Eternal,
The day of march has come!
Henceforth in fields of conquest
Thy tents shall be our home;
Thru days of preparation
Thy grace has made us strong,
And now, O King Eternal,
We lift our battle song.

Lead on, O King Eternal,
Till sin's fierce war shall cease
And holiness shall whisper
The sweet Amen of peace;
For not with swords loud clashing
Nor roll of stirring drums—
With deeds of love and mercy
The heav'nly kingdom comes.

Lead on, O King Eternal,
We follow—not with fears!
For gladness breaks like morning
Where'er Thy face appears;
Thy cross is lifted o'er us,
We journey in its light:
The crown awaits the conquest—
Lead on, O God of might.

Lead On, O King Eternal

I have fought the good fight, I have finished the race, I have kept the faith. Now there is in store for me the crown of righteousness, which the Lord, the righteous Judge, will award to me on that day—and not only to me, but also to all who have longed for his appearing.

—2 Timothy 4:7–8

"Lead On, O King Eternal" was written in 1887 by a young graduating seminarian, Ernest W. Shurtleff. His classmates at Andover Theological Seminary, recognizing their colleague's poetic ability, asked him to write a hymn that they might all sing together for the commencement service. Shurtleff responded with this excellent text. At the time of his graduation he had already published two volumes of verse, and throughout his later ministry he wrote a number of additional hymns. This is his one hymn, however, that has endured with the passing of time.

Following his graduation from Andover Seminary, Ernest Shurtleff served with distinction in Congregational churches in California, Massachusetts, and Minnesota. During this time he was awarded the Doctor of Divinity Degree from Ripon College in Wisconsin, in recognition of his outstanding pulpit ministries.

In 1905, Dr. Shurtleff and his family moved to Europe, where he organized the American Church in Frankfurt, Germany. Later, in Paris, he carried on a remarkable ministry with students and did "deeds of love and mercy" with the poor and needy of that city. It was often said that his entire life was the epitome of the text he had written many years earlier.

On August 24, 1917, at the age of fifty-five, and at the very height of his fruitful ministry in Paris, Ernest Shurtleff was called to his heavenly home to receive the "crown [that] awaits the conquest."

The well-suited martial music for this text was borrowed from a tune written fifty-two years earlier by a noted nineteenth-century English organist and composer, Henry Smart. Smart was well known throughout England as a conductor and compiler of sacred music, even though he spent the last fifteen years of his life in total blindness. Another of Henry Smart's familiar tunes is heard each Christmas season in the hymn "Angels, from the Realms of Glory."

Although the word pictures in this hymn were intended to challenge the graduating class of 1887 at Andover Seminary, the truths can be applied to our lives today. This is not the time for any of us to slacken our efforts in the service of our Lord. "The crown awaits the conquest—Lead on, O God of might."

Somewhere the world has a place for you that is all your own;
Somewhere is work that your hand can do, and yours alone.
Whether afar over land and sea or close at your door may the duty be,
It calls for your service full and free—
Take your place!

—Author Unknown

Thanksgiving Day

~

When we acknowledge God's goodness and faithfulness, we are able to offer Him praise regardless of the circumstances.

—Author Unknown

Thanksgiving Day is one of America's most distinctive holidays, when the people of our land pause to express their gratitude to God for all of His provisions enjoyed individually and as a nation.

> O God, beneath Thy guiding hand
> Our exiled fathers crossed the sea;
> And where they trod the wintry strand
> With prayer and psalm they worshiped Thee.
>
> —Leonard Bacon

In 1624, the General Assembly of Virginia proclaimed March 22 as a day of thanksgiving, commemorating the colony's survival in the 1622 Indian massacre and war. In 1789, following America's victorious revolution, President George Washington in his inaugural address issued the following proclamation:

It is the duty of nations to acknowledge the providence of Almighty God, to obey His will, to be grateful for His benefits, and humbly implore His protection and favor. . . .

124

In 1863, President Abraham Lincoln proclaimed that the last Thursday of November was to be Thanksgiving Day:

> It should be a time when Americans celebrate the plentiful yield of the soil ... the beauty of our land ... the preservation of those ideals of liberty and justice that form the basis of our national life and the hope of international peace.

A presidential proclamation has since become an annual tradition. In December 1941, Congress formalized the Thanksgiving Day observance with a resolution that permanently placed the holiday on the fourth Thursday of each November.

> The worship most acceptable to God comes from a thankful and cheerful heart.
>
> —Plutarch

Prayer

Our Father in Heaven, let not the beauty of this day, or the glow of good health, or the present prosperity of our undertakings deceive us into a false reliance upon our own strength. You have given us every good thing. You have given us life itself with whatever talents we possess ... may we use them wisely. We ask in the name of Jesus Christ our Lord. Amen.

—Peter Marshall

And let there be praise!

Come, ye thankful people, come—
Raise the song of harvest home:
All is safely gathered in
Ere the winter storms begin.
God, our Maker, doth provide
For our wants to be supplied:
Come to God's own temple, come—
Raise the song of harvest home.

All the world is God's own field,
Fruit unto His praise to yield:
Wheat and tares together sown,
Unto joy or sorrow grown.
First the blade and then the ear,
Then the full corn shall appear:
Lord of harvest, grant that we
Wholesome grain and pure may be.

For the Lord our God shall come
And shall take His harvest home:
From His field shall in that day
All offenses purge away—
Give His angels charge at last
In the fire the tares to cast,
But the fruitful ears to store
In His garner evermore.

Even so, Lord, quickly come
To Thy final harvest home:
Gather Thou Thy people in,
Free from sorrow, free from sin;
There, forever purified,
In Thy presence to abide:
Come, with all Thine angels, come—
Raise the glorious harvest home.

Come, Ye
Thankful People

It is a good thing to give thanks unto the LORD, and to sing praises
unto thy name, O most High: to shew forth thy lovingkindness in the
morning, and thy faithfulness every night.

—Psalm 92:1–2 (KJV)

*T*he author of "Come, Ye Thankful People," Henry Alford, is
regarded as one of the most gifted Christian leaders of the nineteenth century, distinguishing himself as a theologian, scholar,
writer, poet, artist, and musician.

Upon graduation in 1832 from Trinity College, Cambridge,
Alford began his public ministry in London. He rose rapidly from
one position to another until he was named Dean of Canter-
bury, the "mother church" of all England. He accepted this pres-
tigious position at the age of forty-seven and kept it until his
death in 1871. It was as a Greek scholar that Dean Alford
attained his greatest distinction. His four-volume edition of the
Greek Testament, on which he labored for twenty years, became
the standard commentary of the latter nineteenth century. As a
member of the New Testament Revision Committee, Alford made
a notable contribution to biblical knowledge on both sides of
the Atlantic.

Hymnology was one of Henry Alford's major interests. He
translated and composed numerous hymns, which he published
in his *Psalms and Hymns* (1844), *The Year of Praise* (1867), and

Poetical Works (1868). Of these many publications, only "Come, Ye Thankful People" is still included in most church hymnals.

This hymn first appeared in Alford's *Psalms and Hymns*. It was originally titled "After Harvest" and was accompanied by the text, "He that goeth forth and weepeth, bearing precious seed, shall doubtless come again with rejoicing, bringing his sheaves with him" (Ps. 126:6 KJV).

The first stanza of this harvest hymn is an invitation and an exhortation to give thanks to God in the earthly temple—His church—for the heavenly care and provision of our earthly needs. The following two stanzas are an interesting commentary on the parable of the wheat and the tares recorded in Matthew 13:24–30, 36–43. The final stanza is a prayer for the Lord's return—"the final harvest home"—the culminating event that Henry Alford saw as the ultimate demonstration of God's goodness in His eternal plan of man's redemption.

The composer of the "St. George's Windsor" tune was George J. Elvey, who served as the organist for forty-seven years at the historic royal chapel at Windsor Castle in England. He was knighted in 1871 for his years of faithful service to the royal family as well as for his many musical publications.

It is said that at the end of a hard day's work as well as after every meal, it was a customary practice for Dean Alford to stand to his feet and offer thanks to God for the blessings just received or enjoyed during the day. This spirit of perpetual gratitude is clearly evidenced throughout this hymn and serves as a model for each of us.

> A thankful heart is not only the greatest virtue, but the parent of all other virtues.
>
> —Cicero

*Great is Thy faithfulness, O God my
Father!
There is no shadow of turning with Thee;
Thou changest not, Thy compassions,
they fail not:
As Thou hast been Thou forever wilt be.*

*CHORUS:
Great is Thy faithfulness!
Great is Thy faithfulness!
Morning by morning new mercies I see;
All I have needed Thy hand hath
provided—
Great is Thy faithfulness, Lord, unto me!*

*Summer and winter, and springtime
and harvest,
Sun, moon and stars in their courses
above,
Join with all nature in manifold witness
To Thy great faithfulness, mercy and love.*

*Pardon for sin and a peace that endureth,
Thine own dear presence to cheer and
to guide,
Strength for today and bright hope for
tomorrow—
Blessings all mine, with ten thousand
beside!*

Great Is Thy Faithfulness

> Because of the
> LORD's great love we are not consumed,
> for his compassions never fail.
> They are new every morning;
> great is your faithfulness.
>
> —Lamentations 3:22–23

*O*ne of the thrilling attributes of God's character is His immutability—*God cannot change!* Of the many hymns written on the theme of God's goodness and faithfulness, "Great Is Thy Faithfulness" stands out like a beacon light. Whereas many hymns are born out of tragedy or some dramatic experience, this hymn was simply the result of the author's "morning by morning" realization of God's personal faithfulness in his daily life. Shortly before his death in 1960, author Thomas Chisholm wrote:

> My income has never been large at any time due to impaired health in the earlier years, which has followed me on until now. But I must not fail to record here the unfailing faithfulness of a covenant keeping God and that He has given me many wonderful displays of His providing care which have filled me with astonishing gratefulness.

From a humble beginning in the log cabin where he was raised in Franklin, Kentucky, and without the benefit of high school or advanced education, Thomas Obediah Chisholm became recognized as one of the important twentieth-century gospel hymn writers. He wrote more than twelve hundred poems, many of which appeared in such religious periodicals as the *Sunday School Times, Moody Monthly,* and the *Alliance Weekly.* A number of these poems have since become prominent hymn texts, including such favorites as "Living for Jesus," "O to Be Like Thee," and "He Was Wounded for Our Transgressions."

What is it about a hymn like "Great Is Thy Faithfulness" that ministers so meaningfully to God's people? Perhaps it is because each us of has those special times in our lives when we are forced to review the good as well as the difficult things that have occurred, and we simply must respond with overwhelming gratitude— "Great is Thy faithfulness, Lord, unto me."

> Good when He gives, supremely good, nor less when He denies;
> Even crosses from His sovereign hand are blessings in disguise.
> —Author Unknown

Or perhaps it is when we have an occasion to enjoy the sights of nature during the changing seasons of the year that we are awed by God's majesty, and we realize anew that even all nature gives "manifold witness to Thy great faithfulness, mercy and love."

> His hand pours beauty from a shining cup upon green hills
> and leafy mountain ways;
> That I may pause in wonder, looking up—and worship Him
> through all my length of days.
> —Author Unknown

And then I realize that this great sovereign of the universe is my personal Savior, my Friend, and my Guide throughout this life and for all eternity. "Blessings all mine, with ten thousand beside!"

> How wonderful to lay my hand in Thine, dear Lord, today;
> And with complete assurance walk with Thee life's unknown way.

—Author Unknown

Thanks be to God for his indescribable gift!

—2 Corinthians 9:15

Christmas Day

~

The Word became flesh and made his dwelling among us.

—John 1:14

*O*ne of the interesting aspects of the American celebration of Christmas is the blending of many traditions from various cultural backgrounds. It makes this the most joyous of all holidays. For Christians, however, Christmas is much more than merely a festive occasion. It is a time of grateful reflection about the most profound truth ever known: The Sovereign of the universe left heaven's glory to be born as an infant in order to become man's Savior and Redeemer. Who can fathom this amazing truth?

With the birth of the Christ Child, the dating of history was completely changed. The years preceding His birth were designated B.C. (before Christ), and the years that followed became A.D. (*anno Domini*— "in the year of the Lord"). The exact date of Jesus' birth is uncertain. The Romans at the time of Jesus had a celebration called Saturnalia, honoring the planet Saturn. They believed that Saturn was the god of the sun and was responsible for all living things. This celebration occurred on December 25. As the worship of the sun became increasingly popular, December 25 grew in importance for the Romans. Later, as the Christian movement grew in numbers, Pope Julius I decreed in about

A.D. 356 that the celebration of Christ's birth and the worship of the sun should be observed jointly on December 25.

In the seventeenth century, when the Puritans realized that the celebration of Christ's birth had at one time been a mixture of paganism and Christianity, they became so dismayed that in 1644 they abolished all Christmas celebrations. After the restoration of the English monarchy, however, the Christmas celebrations were also restored with even more elaborateness. In 1831, Christmas was first declared a legal holiday in the United States.

One of the aspects of Christmas that is enjoyed by nearly everyone is the music of the season. Some of the very finest music known, both sacred and secular, is performed during this time. The singing of our favorite carols in church, home, and school is always enriching to our lives. Somehow, these singable, heartfelt songs have a way of directing our focus on Bethlehem's manger, despite the glitter and commercialism that would otherwise dominate.

The hinge of history is on the door of a Bethlehem stable.
—Ralph W. Stockman

Prayer

Yet doth the star of Bethlehem shed a luster pure and sweet;
And still it leads, as once it led, to the Messiah's feet.
O Father, may that holy star glow every year more bright,
And send its glorious beams afar to fill the world with light.
Amen.

—William Cullen Bryant

And let there be praise!

Joy to the world! the Lord is come;
Let earth receive her King.
Let ev'ry heart prepare Him room,
And heav'n and nature sing,
And heav'n and nature sing,
And heav'n, and heav'n and nature sing.

Joy to the world! the Savior reigns;
Let men their songs employ,
While fields and floods, rocks, hills and
plains
Repeat the sounding joy,
Repeat the sounding joy,
Repeat, repeat the sounding joy.

No more let sin and sorrow grow,
Nor thorns infest the ground.
He comes to make His blessings flow
Far as the curse is found,
Far as the curse is found,
Far as, far as the curse is found.

He rules the world with truth and grace,
And makes the nations prove
The glories of His righteousness,
And wonders of His love,
And wonders of His love,
And wonders, and wonders of His love.

Joy to the World

Shout for joy to the LORD, all the earth,
burst into jubilant song with music.

—Psalm 98:4

*J*oy is the keynote of the Christmas season. The long-awaited one has come to earth to live among us. Let us shout for joy to the Lord. "Joy to the World" is one of the most joyous Christmas hymns in existence, not in the sense of merrymaking but in the solemn realization of what Christ's birth has meant to mankind.

This carol is another of Isaac Watts's hymns from his well-known hymnal of 1719, *Psalms of David Imitated in the Language of the New Testament.* It was his intent to give the psalms a New Testament meaning and style. "Joy to the World" is a paraphrase of these verses taken from the last half of Psalm 98:

Make a joyful noise unto the LORD, all the earth: make a loud noise, and rejoice, and sing praise.... Let the floods clap their hands: let the hills be joyful together before the LORD; for he cometh to judge the earth: with righteousness shall he judge the world, and the people with equity.

—verses 4, 8–9 (KJV)

Psalm 98 is a Jewish song of rejoicing at the marvelous ways in which God has protected and restored His chosen people. The psalm anticipates the time when Jehovah will be the God of the whole earth and Israel's law will be accepted by all the nations.

However, Isaac Watts has given the psalm a fresh interpretation: a New Testament expression of praise for the salvation that began when God became incarnate as the babe of Bethlehem and was destined to remove the curse of Adam's fall. Watts first titled his text "The Messiah's Coming and Kingdom."

In all, Isaac Watts wrote more than six hundred hymns throughout his lifetime. Because of his bold departure from the traditional psalms and later the introduction of his "hymns of human composure"—texts based solely on one's own thoughts and words—Watts was considered by many in his day to be a radical churchman. More than two and one-half centuries later, however, our hymnals still contain many of his beloved songs of praise, and he is respectfully known as the "father of the English hymn." Many students of hymnody would also readily agree that Isaac Watts was the greatest hymn writer of all time.

In 1836, Lowell Mason, an American choir director, composer, and public school educator, was thought to have rearranged a portion of the music of Handel's *Messiah,* likely from some of the phrases in the numbers "Comfort Ye" and "Lift Up Your Heads," to fit Watts's "Joy to the World" text. This adapted tune became known as the "Antioch" tune; it first appeared in Lowell Mason's *Modern Psalmist* in 1839.

Through the combined talents of an English literary genius of the eighteenth century, a German-born musical giant from the same period, and a nineteenth-century American choir director and educator, another great hymn was born that has since found a permanent place in the pages of church hymnals for use during every Christmas season.

I bring you good news of great joy that will be for all the people. Today in the town of David a Savior has been born to you; he is Christ the Lord.

—Luke 2:10–11

What Child is this, Who, laid to rest
On Mary's lap is sleeping?
Whom angels greet with anthems sweet,
While shepherds watch are keeping?

REFRAIN
This, this is Christ the King;
Whom shepherds guard and angels sing:
Haste, haste to bring Him laud,
The Babe, the Son of Mary!

Why lies He in such mean estate,
Where ox and ass are feeding?
Good Christian, fear: for sinners here
The silent Word is pleading:

So bring Him incense, gold, and myrrh,
Come peasant, king to own Him,
The King of kings salvation brings;
Let loving hearts enthrone Him.

What Child Is This?

When they had seen him, they [shepherds] spread the word concerning what had been told them about this child, and all who heard it were amazed.

—Luke 2:17–18

*T*he question posed in this well-loved carol must have been uppermost in the minds of those present at Jesus' birth. We can almost hear the question being asked from one to another as they gazed into the humble manger. How difficult it must have been for them to understand that the Babe who lay in "such mean estate" was truly the long-awaited Messiah. And through the centuries men have continued to ponder who Christ really is: How can He be fully God and still fully man? Only through divine faith comes the revealed answer.

He who is the Bread of Life began His ministry hungering.
He who is the Water of Life ended His ministry thirsty.
Christ hungered as man, yet fed the multitudes as God.
He was led as a lamb to the slaughter, yet He is the Good Shepherd.
He died, and by dying destroyed death.

—Author Unknown

Since the time of Christ's birth, confusion about His identity has continued. One day Jesus asked His disciples this question, "Who do people say the Son of Man is?" The answers were varied: "Some say John the Baptist; others say Elijah; and still others,

Jeremiah or one of the prophets," responded the disciples. Then Jesus asked the all-important question that every individual in life must answer: "But what about you? . . . Who do you say I am?" (Matt. 16:13–15).

How forcefully the triumphant answer to this imposing question bursts forth in the hymn's refrain—"This, this is Christ the King."

The hymn's thoughtful text was written by William C. Dix, who was one of our finest lay hymn writers. As a successful insurance administrator in Glasgow, Scotland, Dix was stricken suddenly with a serious illness at the age of twenty-nine. He was confined to bed for an extended period and suffered deep depression until he called out to God and "met Him in a new and real way." Out of this spiritual experience came more than forty artistic and distinctive hymns, including this delightful carol. It was taken from a longer Christmas poem, "The Manger Throne," written by Dix in 1865. Another of his well-known Christmas hymns is "As with Gladness Men of Old."

The melody "Greensleeves" is a traditional English folk tune of unknown origin. Through the years it has been associated with a great variety of texts. William Shakespeare noted in some of his plays that "Greensleeves" was a favorite tune of his day.

> Who is He in yonder stall,
> At whose feet the shepherds fall?
> 'Tis the Lord! O wondrous story!
> 'Tis the Lord! The King of Glory!

At His feet we humbly fall.
Crown Him! Crown Him! Lord of All!

—Benjamin R. Hanby

To the Seeker . . . Christ is the way,
To the Philosopher . . . Christ is the truth,
To the Penitent . . . Christ is the life.

—Author Unknown

Yet to all who received him, to those who believed in his name,
he gave the right to become children of God.

—John 1:12

REFRAIN
Go, tell it on the mountain,
Over the hills and ev'rywhere—
Go, tell it on the mountain
That Jesus Christ is born!

While shepherds kept their watching
O'er silent flocks by night,
Behold, thruout the heavens
There shone a holy light.

The shepherds feared and trembled
When lo! above the earth
Rang out the angel chorus
That hailed our Savior's birth.

Down in a lowly manger
The humble Christ was born,
And God sent us salvation
That blessed Christmas morn.

Go, Tell It on the Mountain

> You who bring good tidings to Zion,
> go up on a high mountain.
> You who bring good tidings to Jerusalem,
> lift up your voice with a shout,
> lift it up, do not be afraid;
> say to the towns of Judah,
> "Here is your God!"
>
> —Isaiah 40:9

A story to tell, a song to be sung, a message to give, a Savior to show, a gospel to proclaim as well as demonstrate.

Christmas, for Christians, is much more than a once-a-year celebration. It is a fresh awareness that a Deliverer was sent from heaven's glory to become personally involved in the redemption and affairs of the human race.

> Out of the ivory palaces, into a world of woe,
> Only His great, eternal love made my Savior go.
> —Henry Barraclough

The impact of this realization becomes a compelling motive to share the thrilling message that "God sent us salvation that blessed Christmas morn."

From a background of oppressive slavery, dating back to the early seventeenth century, came a wealth of songs that formerly were known as "Negro spirituals," but now are most often simply called "spirituals." They remain one of the finest bodies of folk music found anywhere in the world. In the midst of their cruel circumstances, the slaves turned to Christianity and the promise that Scripture gave of One who would be a Guide and Friend for eternity. During the latter part of the eighteenth and early nineteenth centuries there was an earnest attempt by many southern churches to evangelize the slaves. This was a time when the spirituals began to flourish. However, few of these songs were collected or published prior to about 1840.

Like most spirituals, the refrain for "Go, Tell It on the Mountain" is anonymous. Spirituals, for the most part, simply evolved out of community life and worship. They seldom had just one author or composer. Different individuals added verses and musical embellishments as a song was used. The stanzas for this spiritual were written by John W. Work Jr., a professor at Fisk University. He and his brother, Frederick J. Work, were early leaders in spreading and promoting the popularity of spirituals.

From 1871 to 1875, the Jubilee Singers of Fisk University toured the United States and Europe extensively to introduce spirituals to large audiences for the first time. In 1907, the songs first appeared in published form in Frederick J. Work's book, *Folk Songs of the American Negroes.* "Go, Tell It on the Mountain" is from that collection. It is no doubt the best known of all Christmas spirituals.

These traditional spirituals have become an important part of the American folk and sacred music heritage and are greatly appreciated and enjoyed by all of God's people.

This is the month, and this the happy morn,
Wherein the Son of Heaven's eternal King,
Of wedded maid and virgin mother born,
Our great redemption from above did bring;
For so the holy sages once did sing,
That He our deadly forfeit should release,
And with His Father work us a perpetual peace.

—John Milton

Then the glory of the LORD will be revealed,
And all flesh will see it together;
For the mouth of the LORD has spoken.

—Isaiah 40:5 (NASB)

Amazing Grace—gift edition
Illustrated Stories of Favorite Hymns

This colorful illustrated edition includes 28 of the most popular hymn story devotionals from the best-selling *Amazing Grace.* Songs include "Great Is Thy Faithfulness," "Holy, Holy, Holy," and "It Is Well with My Soul."